POSTMODERNISM
AND THE SEARCH FOR
ENLIGHTENMENT

POSTMODERNISM
AND THE SEARCH FOR
ENLIGHTENMENT

Karlis Racevskis

University Press of Virginia

CHARLOTTESVILLE AND LONDON

THE UNIVERSITY PRESS OF VIRGINIA
Copyright © 1993
by the Rector and Visitors
of the University of Virginia

First published 1993

Library of Congress
Cataloging-in-Publication Data

Racevskis, Karlis.
 Postmodernism and the search for
enlightenment / Karlis Racevskis.
     p.   cm.
 Includes bibliographical references and
index.
   ISBN 0-8139-1471-X
   1. Postmodernism.   2. Enlightenment.
 3. Humanities.   I. Title.
 B831.2.R33   1933
 190—dc20   93-7338
                                    CIP

Printed in the United States of America

For Maija

and the crew:
Laila
Roland
Andrew

CONTENTS

PREFACE

THE DECADE OF THE SIXTIES produced a theoretical explosion in the humanities in whose aftermath we are still embroiled. We have witnessed the emergence of critical discourses that can take on a variety of resonances; they can sound apocalyptic or hopeful, they can appear nihilistic or utopian, and they can elicit contradictory, sometimes enthusiastic, sometimes violently negative reactions. The proliferation of these discourses, their intensity, their extraordinary capacity for proselytizing as well as for creating resentment and suspicion—are all aspects that point to the symptomatic significance of the phenomenon. What is especially noteworthy is that the concern with critical theory has spilled over academic boundaries and has been attracting the attention of politicians, government officials, members of the media and, as a consequence, the general public.

As some critics have noted, the university—or, more exactly, the humanities—have become a veritable battlefield. Indeed, the rhetoric of the contestants and of the journalists is rife with the imagery of war; there is much talk of invasions, sieges, battles, attacks, counteroffensives. On the one hand, we may well find it ironic that the university, and even more the humanities, should have become the focus of so much concern and the pretext for such animosity. On the other, while there is clearly a good deal of bombast and posturing in the public pronouncements of the spokespersons for the various factions and while members of the press have blown up the crisis in their journalistic fashion, there is no denying a feeling of uneasiness, of disarray and disaffection marking the practice of the humanities today.

Yet there is also a more positive aspect to this story: there is a sense of renewed purpose and intensity in the air; it is a time when the study of the humanities seems crucial once more, when stu-

dents and professors feel energized by the debates and the controversies. What is at issue, many of us would like to think, is something that is hardly academic anymore and we are beginning to
suspect that the current debates concern a fundamental reorientation in our ways of seeing and understanding our society and of
gauging the prospects for our civilization.

While for some observers the current juncture forebodes im-
pending chaos and security is to be sought in a retreat to the psychic
comforts offered by basic values and traditional disciplines, for
others, the promise of chaos is itself a hopeful prospect and offers a
welcome contrast to the bad faith and delusions fostered by traditional metaphysical thinking. From the perspective of others still,
the bad faith is exemplified by those who hold to such romantic
anarchistic schemes and who refuse to see that their critique is made
possible by the privileged position they enjoy in a culture selling
comfort and favoring the comfortable. My book is an attempt to
survey the debates and sort out some of these issues.

One of the themes that unifies these contradictory approaches is
a sometimes explicit, sometimes implicit, attempt to come to grips
with the yet unfulfilled promise of the Enlightenment. This is not
something I claim to have discovered; the theme of Enlightenment
has been a central component in debates opposing modernists to
postmodernists, Marxists to post-Marxists, liberals to conservatives. My contribution is to have juxtaposed a number of the
arguments in the hope of placing some of the issues in a new light.
For this purpose, I have availed myself of a number of theoretical
models. The principal influence has been that of Michel Foucault,
but there are quite a few other thinkers from whose work I have
profited and whose influence I consider to have been salutary in the
current critical debates. More than at any other time in history
perhaps, intellectual work today is implicated in a general, constantly evolving project that is sustained by the efforts of numerous
contributors sharing similar concerns.

This fairly eclectic aspect of my approach reflects my own research projects—articles, book reviews, papers written over the
last decade. It is a period of time during which I have benefited
from a number of fortuitous circumstances and fortunate acquain-
tances. I therefore wish to thank Wright State University for granting me a sabbatical and a research leave and for otherwise gener-

ously supporting my endeavors. I feel especially indebted to Anni Whissen, who chairs the Department of Modern Languages there, for her steadfast and enthusiastic support. I must also thank the Commonwealth Center for Literary and Cultural Change at the University of Virginia for a fellowship that gave me the opportunity to pursue my work under circumstances and in an atmosphere that I can only term ideal. I am particularly grateful to the Center's director, Ralph Cohen, whose guidance and example were an inspiration to all participants.

I also wish to mention the influence of GRIP—the Group for Research into the Institutionalization and Professionalization of literary studies. Many of the issues I raise came into focus in the course of the remarkably collegial and always lively exchanges organized under the auspices of GRIP.

This is not to say that my work intends to reflect some consensus or reproduce a well-defined position. While the critical project in which many are taking part today is occasionally characterized as an enterprise epitomizing the general deterioration of the Western value system, it by no means imposes a uniformity of views or some kind of allegiance to a common cause. Far from helping to establish some tyrannical form of political correctness, it precludes the hope of ever arriving at comfortable, definitive resolutions of the dilemmas of cultural criticism; indeed, the postmodern critical strategy is one that ceaselessly impels thinking toward new areas of investigation, to ever-different realms of uncertainty. The force of this postmodern lucidity postpones the comforts of commonly shared solutions to the dilemmas besetting our time as it highlights an insuperable obligation to confront the unknown our age discovers to have shaped its claims to certitude.

Finally, I would like to express my appreciation for the editorial help and guidance provided by the University Press of Virginia. I am especially grateful for the judicious comments and valuable suggestions made by the two anonymous readers of my manuscript. Needless to say, the responsibility for any remaining shortcomings is mine alone.

I have used previously published materials by excerpting, rewriting, and translating, passages from the following articles and book reviews: "Re(dis)covering Structuralism," *Diacritics* 14, no. 4

(1984): 37–46. "Lacan et l'histoire du structuralisme: les ambiguités d'une définition," *Analytica* 39 (1984): 55–61. "The Structuralist Legacy: The Story of a Literary Misunderstanding," *Works and Days* 5 (1985): 39–50. "Le dilemme des humanités aux USA: une perspective structuraliste," *Bulletin de liaison* (Université de Lyon 2) 2 (1985): 3–12. "The Critique of Poststructuralism and the Revival of Eurocentric Thought," *Works and Days* 9 (Spring 1987): 65–72. "The Modernity of *Moralistes* and the (A)Morality of Postmodernists," *Antioch Review* 45 (Summer 1987): 275–79. "Michel Foucault, Rameau's Nephew, and the Question of Identity," *Philosophy and Social Criticism* 12 (Summer 1987): 132–44. "The Gap in the Humanities," *Critical Exchange,* no. 23 (Summer 1987): 65–75. "Le discours postmoderne et la crise des humanités aux Etats-Unis," *Bulletin de liaison* (Université de Lyon 2) 10 (Feb. 1988): 3–11. "The Conative Function of the Other in *Les mots et les choses,*" *Revue internationale de philosophie* 173 (1990): 231–40. "Post-Foucaldian Strategies," *Poetics Today* 12 (1991): 347–62. "Michel Foucault and the Second Coming," *Radical Philosophy* 57 (Spring 1991): 50–53. "The Political Implications of Foucault's Philosophy," *Bulletin de la Société Américaine de Philosophie de Langue Française* 3, no. 1 (1991): 5–11. "De l'homme soviétique à l'homme postmoderne: réflexion sur un passage politico-culturel," *Bulletin de liaison* (Université de Lyon 2) 16 (Spring 1991): 3–12. Chapter 4 is an expanded version of an article that first appeared in *Papers on Language and Literature* 29, no. 1 (1993).

POSTMODERNISM
AND THE SEARCH FOR
ENLIGHTENMENT

INTRODUCTION

THE PARADIGM OF Western thought known as modernity is unraveling. In fact, modernity has been unraveling for some time, but
signs of the disintegration have been especially noticeable of late
and can be observed in almost all areas of intellectual and artistic
activity. The crisis undergone by modernity has therefore called
attention to the phenomenon of modernity itself. Moreover, as its
hold over us loosens, this pattern or habit of thought becomes
more and more accessible to analysis and critique. We are thus in a
position not only to grasp the very concept of modernity but, more
important, to see that its dissolution was made inevitable by a flaw
attributable to its very core and essence.

Viewed from the perspective of this dissolution, modernity appears both as a conceit and a coherence: it was sustained from the
first by the self-satisfied claim of objective knowledge and systematic understanding that helped place the concept of Western
"man" in charge of the destiny of all humankind. Paradoxically, it
is at the very moment when the Western *ratio* appears to have
reached its fulfillment in the hegemonic application of technoscien-
tific thought that its fundamental incapacity for realizing its aims
has been revealed. As the philosopher Dominique Janicaud points
out, "The world has never been so rationalized; reason has never
been so impotent."[1] The cause for the failure turns out to be very
simple: the *reason* Western "man" has used since the eighteenth
century both to found and legitimate his understanding of reality is
increasingly incapable of accounting for the complexity it uncovers
and for the causality it purports to explain.

To be sure, the campaign against reason has a long and distinguished history. Reason's reasons were being questioned already in
the eighteenth century by such thinkers as Diderot and Rousseau.
This critique was taken up in the nineteenth notably by Marx,

Nietzsche, and Freud. The will to discredit what has been called the "Cartesian-Kantian paradigm" intensified in our century, and attempts to list these subversive influences inevitably produce an impressive array of the most eminent thinkers in twentieth-century Western philosophy. Thus, according to one such enumeration, "the devastating critiques in the twentieth century by Charles Peirce, William James, Alfred North Whitehead, John Dewey, W. V. Quine, Wilfred Sellars, Nelson Goodman, Hilary Putnam and Richard Rorty in the United States; Martin Heidegger, Hans-Georg Gadamer and the Frankfurt School theorists in Germany; J. L. Austin and Gilbert Ryle in England; Merleau-Ponty, Lucien Goldmann, Jacques Derrida, and Michel Foucault in France; Georg Lukács in Hungary; and Ludwig Wittgenstein of Austria, all leave the Cartesian-Kantian picture in shambles."[2]

The campaign against reason has become especially telling of late. It has been associated, in particular, with the work of the French structuralists and poststructuralists. Also to be noted is the essential contribution of feminist criticism, which has done much to reveal reason's complicity with masculine norms and interests. In addition, the hollowness of reason's claims has become evident in a number of domains over which it had established its prerogative. In the humanities, the canonical status of Western "man's" thought has been shaken by the newly discovered legitimacy of works by women, members of ethnic minorities, and Third World authors. In the realm of politics, the self-assurance with which decisions are made has been undermined by the realization, noted in a recent issue of *Le Monde diplomatique,* that "any decision, whatever it may be, will be related to a wager because it will be impossible to make it rationally, with a cool head, after an exact evaluation of its consequences; furthermore, any initiative, no matter how reasonable it might at first appear, will inevitably impose on humanity a new dose of suffering." It is important to note, however, that these disclosures have not necessarily ensued in apathy or resignation but have brought about the understanding that, in most cases of active intervention in world affairs, "only a preventive medicine would have been able to spare the world another dose of trials."[3] Indeed, one of today's most promising strategies for dealing with cultural and political realities consists of emphasizing the preventive at the expense of the instrumental application of reason. This procedure, which could well be called postmodern, amounts to a weakening of reason, and is achieved, principally, by means of a deconstruction of reason's motives.

This backing away from the forceful claims of the traditional model of reason achieves several beneficial results: it averts the delusions and abuses made possible by an unquestioned reliance on instrumental reason and it permits the establishment of a critical distance with regard to the central driving force of modernity, a perspective that allows for a reexamination of modernity's rise and of the sources of its hegemony. It is a strategic retreat made necessary by an understanding that is characteristic of postmodern thinking, namely, that modernity cannot be confronted head-on and with its own devices; for example, it cannot be overcome or surpassed since overcoming and surpassing are the very themes that have given modernity its power and appeal. Nor can it be overcome by unreason, for example. It is therefore necessary to find another form of reason, a new kind of rational approach initiated from what the French feminist philosopher Michèle LeDœuff describes as "a position where the alternative between hegemonic reason and a revolt of unreason can be seen as mythical, a connivance or complicity between forms which present themselves as opposites." Such a position would be crucial in a strategy aimed at disarming, invalidating current systems of domination and their attendant networks of power. As LeDœuff notes wryly, it is, after all, "being a little too generous always to credit power with the privilege of reason."[4] As a result of such an approach, a reversal occurs; while the Enlightenment handed down the belief that reason legitimates power—indeed, that reason is power—we are now able to appreciate the extent to which it is power that gives reason its prerogatives, that power, in short, produces the reason—or reasons—it needs.

The disenchantment with out civilization's failure to realize the aspirations of the Enlightenment is of course not new. This theme is most readily associated with the Frankfurt School of critics and with the work of Adorno and Horkheimer in particular; their well-known critical concept of the "dialectic of the Enlightenment" has helped explain how the liberating potential of reason has effectively been negated by the institutions and social structures put in place in the nineteenth century. Their argument proposed that "reason did not necessarily produce rationality; on the contrary, the very project of rational control, while other social relations remained unchanged, produced unreason." As a result of this basic flaw in the Enlightenment project, the alleged emancipation of "Man" was also accompanied by the development of a "manipulative, instrumental reason."[5]

The suspicion that reason may have served as a convenient cover for processes and programs that had their own reasons and interests is also characteristic of the work of the French structuralist and poststructuralist writers. The critique of reason becomes, for them, a component of a more general attack against the philosophy of humanism—a form of rationality whose elaboration is seen to accompany the development of certain strategies of political power in the nineteenth century. One of the main accomplishments of this critique has been to show that, while Enlightenment thought had effectively eliminated God as the effective guarantee for validating knowledge, it had retained the basic principles of a theonomous orientation: reason maintained its ascendancy on the basis of a totalizing and universalizing view of human experience. This view brought with it an important and inescapable corollary: it validated an autonomous source of thought. It legitimated a logic of identity that posited the world in terms of a willful and responsible consciousness enjoying a transitive relationship with reality. One of the notable achievements of the structuralist project is the attention it brought to bear on the concept of the subject. The latter became a central theme in the theoretical investigations carried out in the sixties, a time when "philosophers, sociologists, psychoanalysts, linguists converge to proclaim that the myth of the subject's autonomy has conveniently made it possible to submerge in nebulousness the networks of structures that shape and constrain culture, secrete the imaginary, articulate language, impose norms, interdict thought, diverting it from its object." The theme of a self-sufficient, autonomous, conscious, and purposeful subjective plenitude was also seen as the principle supporting Western civilization's claims of moral superiority and was held responsible for many of the delusions it had fostered: the unquestioned privileged status of the subject had permitted the erection of the vast system called "Western humanism," which frequently turned out to be nothing more than "a screen and an alibi for barbarism."[6]

The theoretical writings of the sixties thus acquired a marked political intent and strove to radically change our understanding of the relationships of power that constitute society. These writings made us realize, for example, that the principle of identity marking the emergence of modern thought was also the driving force of political thinking and that the rationales informing political activity continue to espouse the concept of autonomous agency: "The marriage of the idea of the self and of civil authority propelled the political imagination of the Enlightenment and still characterizes the West today."[7] From the perspective developed by structuralist theorizing, the continuing belief in the autonomy of the thinking subject and in the subject's transitive relationship to the real is simply a well-preserved illusion.

It is also on this score that thinkers such as Foucault and Derrida have encountered the greatest resistance to their ideas. Because they appear to deny the possibility of a conscious and purposeful opposition to oppression, their work as the leading French intellectuals of the sixties has been criticized for being politically ineffective, irrelevant, and for serving the interests of the status quo. Jürgen Habermas, one of the staunchest defenders of modernity and a firm believer in the continuing validity of the Enlightenment project, has thus accused the major French thinkers of the sixties of being neoconservatives. The motive behind the accusation is obvious; Habermas and others who share his viewpoint cannot forgive the French for trying to disrupt the connection linking philosophy to politics and for attempting to discredit the claims made for the progressive, emancipating effects of enlightened action.

Habermas and his followers are having a difficult time in making their case, however. Indeed, their reasoning appears outmoded and, as a number of critics have pointed out, it suffers from a fundamental and debilitating flaw because of its adherence to the metaphysics of traditional Western humanism; thus, the assumption that civilization progresses by dint of a rational purpose has yet to be substantiated: "This criticism of the postmodern *dissolution* of the bond between modern rationality and societal modernization depends, of course, upon the assumption that the bond is real."[8] Clearly, the case for a direct causal link between thought and action, intention and results, reason and progress, political struggle and emancipation has lost much of its credibility. The claim that change can be controlled and brought about through willful, purposeful human agency has become suspect because it assumes the possibility of situating opposition outside the workings of power. What has become increasingly evident is that such an opposition, "beginning as a challenge to the all-embracing or totalising 'identity' of the system of capital, turns out to be itself fully implicated in the production and maintenance of the very principle of identity which it proposes to question."[9] The system in place produces not only domination and oppression but the very conditions making a critique of this domination and oppression possible; the subject is inseparable from power: "Power relations change, shape and produce the very reality we experience (and the 'who' of the 'we' of any particular experience), hence central to modern power is its productivity, not its repressive effects."[10] The important questions for today, as Foucault pointed out, orient our thinking in a radically different direction: "How are we constituted as subjects of our own knowledge? How are we constituted as subjects who exercise or submit to power relations? How are we constituted as moral subjects of our own actions?"[11] The belief that our actions can be guided by truths and knowledge we have acquired before we enter into relations of power is no longer defensible, from a Foucaultian perspective: "Knowledge and truth are no longer for Foucault, as they were for the humanists, the enemies of power, but are absolutely essential to its functioning."[12]

The theoretical production of the structuralist era also has had a profound effect on the conception of the intellectual's role and responsibility. The causal link between philosophical cogency and political effectiveness that was a basic tenet for Enlightenment activism has now been irreparably broken. The traditional models for an intellectual's prerogatives and place in society have lost their relevance in the face of the deep-down realization that the ambitions that grounded the validity of the intellectual mode of life have failed: "There is no would-be enlightened despot seeking the counsel of philosophers. There are only philosophers desperately trying to create communities, and sustain them with the power of their arguments alone."[13] The notion of postmodernism has become a useful concept in this regard; it works as a shorthand specification for the current malaise affecting the kind of artistic, literary, and theoretical activity that seeks to engage culture critically while questioning the purpose and validity of this very activity. But postmodernism is not simply useful for characterizing a current version of a *mal du siècle;* it designates, as well, a whole range of concrete, positive attitudes toward intellectual and artistic activity. First and foremost, the term *postmodernism* stands for a critical strategy.

There are a number of themes that can be considered central to the development of a postmodern critical strategy. The first is, precisely, the critical intent, which can be attributed to a general malaise, a dissatisfaction or alienation experienced vis-à-vis the presently dominating mode of thought—that is, with respect to modernity. Secondly, the critical function of postmodernist thought is determined by its intimate, dependent relation to modernity. This dependency is made inevitable—and explicit—by the term *postmodern* itself, and points to a cause-effect relationship between an age and its aftermath. At the same time, this relationship is critical in intent because postmodernism constitutes itself in terms of a lack or a failure that is seen as inscribed into modernity's very reason for coming into existence. There are important consequences to this realization. Taken as a critical mode then, postmodernism can be considered not only as a tendency well within modernity itself but one present at the moment of modernity's inception. As a result, its success—measured by the ever-growing following postmodern theories are gaining—can only bring its own demise; but it also can be taken as a symptom of modernity's extenuation. From the perspective of a postmodern critique, this extenuation points to modernity's signal failure to fulfill the promise of the Enlightenment and underlines the necessity to dismantle the Cartesian-Kantian paradigm in order to clear the ground for a different mode of thought. The aim of the postmodern critical project is thus to rethink our relations with the world by doing away, as much as possible, with those metaphysical themes that have mainly served to cover up the lack of a legitimate connection between the claims of modernity and the evolution of Western civilization.

A postmodern critique seeks to invalidate first the pretense of a rational design for humanity carried out under the aegis of a disinterested pursuit of truth. Thus, for Foucault, explanatory schemes that seek to account for social processes and for institutional and human practices in all their complexity can only produce delusions; what characterizes human affairs is not a coherence of aims and achievements but a fundamental "lack of correspondence between programmes, practices and effects."[14] It is clear now that the belief in this correspondence was made possible by the undisputed authority of such universal themes as reason, truth, and progress. As long as it was possible to trust in the power of the enlightened individual to advance the cause of progress and to improve the lot of humankind it was also possible to ignore the material reality of relations of power and their dependence on the very discourses that promised emancipation and equality. Modern "man's" belief in the self-sufficiency of his reasons allowed him to neglect all that escaped the realm of his self-generated and self-validating limitations. By vesting all claims of earthly authority in universal reason, by endowing the knowledge necessary for maintaining a socio-political order with the prestige of truth, the project of civilization could make itself impervious to the rule of contingency and the force of history.

The process is still in place, of course: "The notion that reason is divorced from 'merely contingent' existence still predominates in contemporary Western thought and now appears to mask the embeddedness and dependence of the self upon social relations."[15] But the notion is increasingly coming under attack. Feminist critics, who have been particularly sensitive to the effects of social relations on the reality of subjects, have elaborated telling critiques of the metaphysical alibis that have helped keep existing power structures in place. They are thus contributing the latest and perhaps the most effective chapter in a tactic of unmasking and critical inversion that has operated as the reverse counterpart to modernity's self-assertiveness. By revealing the lack of correspondence between official representations of reality and the effects of institutional and social practices on individual lives, feminist critics have foregrounded the material, lived experience of persons, thus freeing it from the kind of universalizing themes used to lock individuals within the confines of imaginary representations. The meaning of existence is no longer to be found in the telos of a historical promise or the fulfillment of a human essence-to-be-fulfilled but in the material conditions of everyday reality. Values are declared to be without foundation, not because feminist or postmodernist critics are inveterate anarchists or nihilists but because the evidence of a world seen without metaphysically colored glasses has inescapably led to this conclusion: we have come to understand once more what was already evident to a number of philosophes in the eighteenth century, namely, that values are sustained by nothing more than the self-interest of those wishing to promote them.

Understandably, the revelation that there is no causal link between a discourse of human values and the effective workings of power-knowledge networks has caused consternation and uneasiness. In some quarters the reaction has been to shore up the old pretense and to reclaim the high ground of humanist and humanitarian rhetoric. For postmodern critics the task has been to turn the crisis in philosophy into a philosophy of crisis—into a discourse seeking to provide lucidity and to avoid self-referentiality. Postmodernists have been intent on investigating the logical and ethical dilemmas that have emerged on the cultural horizon of modernity and have pursued the paradoxes of the postmodern condition to their aporetic ends. They hope thus to promote an understanding that will prevent them from recycling the familiar pattern of modernity's scheme. By refusing to disinvolve itself from the object of its critique, to claim a separate, superior, unimplicated and uncontaminated position of critical authority, by predicating its critique on a strategy that is self-critical by definition, postmodernism acquires the capacity to disable the recuperative strategies of modernity. It does precisely what modernity failed to carry out when it thought it was eliminating the guarantee of revelation, when it replaced God—one source of transcendental authority—with reason, which was another: it avoids adopting yet another, equally inaccessible, undefinable, and insuperable alibi. It recognizes that the idea of a foundation is itself foundationless, or rather, that it is simply based on the strategic need to claim a foundation. The strategy itself is but a tautological procedure reproducing the Cartesian attempt to posit a subjective plenitude, to demonstrate the truth of a concept whose truth cannot be proved because the very moment "I" declares itself thinking, it exists.[16]

The importance of Descartes's founding role in this tradition can hardly be overstated: "After Descartes's meditations, modern philosophy becomes a philosophy of the subject. As the locus of certainty and truth, subjectivity is the first principle from which everything arises and to which all must be reduced."[17] Ever since Descartes accomplished the conjunction of the epistemological with the ontological, Western "man" has been able to found the truth of his knowledge in the essence of his being. The validity of "man's" thought has been guaranteed by his fundamental nature—he is a rational being. The certitude and righteousness of Western thought is thus founded on an "anthropological substratum" that is no longer possible to ignore; its existence is designated by the very meaning of the word *subject,* which, in its etymological derivation, is to be taken as what lies beneath as a substratum for processes deemed natural. What such a procedure has accomplished is a particular pattern that can be considered characteristic of the modern age: a rational pretense covering up a basically irrational procedure in which the subject is controlled rather than in control. In the wake of structuralist and poststructuralist theorizing, the body of knowledge that mediates between a purposeful consciousness and the world it perceives has been irremediably problematized and the premise that *what* consciousness perceives is very much a function of what it *is* has become axiomatic; the subject of one's perception is understood to be both its object and its origin. The subject of a discourse is just as much the *who* speaks as the *what* is spoken, the who being determined by what one knows—even before one knows it.

The pretense of modernity is collapsing today precisely because the circularity of the tactic upholding its founding themes has become evident, and "if Western reason seems to have exhausted its possibilities, it's because it has always functioned by dint of its own assertivity."[18] The truth of modernity's claims is shown to be based on nothing more than the will to establish this truth. No longer able to claim the prestige of truthfulness, postmodern discourse becomes a Nietzschean way of thinking about error and erring and thus "emphasizes that it is not a question of thinking about the non-true, but rather of examining the process of becoming of the 'false' constructs of metaphysics, morality, religion and art, that is, the entire tissue of erring that alone constitutes the wealth or, more simply put, the *essence* of *reality*."[19] This attempt to constitute a genealogy of our prejudices amounts to a fictionalization of the world and is intended to safeguard discourse from the temptation to again found experience in metaphysical principles. Since truth is contingent and is determined by the sociohistorical circumstances attending its elaboration, what we have left are "different histories or different levels and ways of reconstructing the past in the collective consciousness and imagination."[20] The new critical strategy will therefore be hermeneutical, and instead of seeking to ground itself, it will refer the work of interpretation to commonly shared, contingent epistemological notions and ethical needs—and will not reconstruct meanings by referring them to essences and truths deemed self-evident. To understand how human actions and thinking are constituted is to give meaning not to the activities and intentions of willful and autonomous human subjects but to interpret the discursive practices that mold the subjects and their objects—as well as the relations linking them. What such a perspective proposes is the elaboration of a detailed understanding of the connections between different types of knowledge, between discursive and nondiscursive practices, between regimes of truth and the power networks making them operative. The investigation of these links has led to the deployment of what could be termed counterdisciplinary strategies—of discourses that tend to obliterate the conventional and comfortable distinctions between realms of thought whose identity and autonomy have been deemed essential for the maintenance of a particular rationality or worldview.

To be sure, the status and even the validity of the postmodern critical project are still very much in question. It continues to be accused of collusion with the forces of repression or of decadence in our civilization. But it can also be viewed as a most dynamic and promising development in the practice of the humanities today—if only for its capacity for stirring up controversy. This is also my view; and I believe it is in the confrontation between disciplinary and counterdisciplinary thought that the most useful and innovative thinking is taking place; that it is in the confusion created by the clash of irreconcilables—of reason and unreason, of identity and alterity, of tradition and subversion—that new, more democratic and less exclusive modes of thought find themselves adumbrated.

CHAPTER I

THE POLITICS OF
STRUCTURALIST THOUGHT

IN A PREFACE written for an edition of Voltaire's *Contes philosophiques,* Roland Barthes characterized the author of *Candide* as "the last of the happy writers." This happiness was possible, says Barthes, because the philosophe saw himself struggling against an enemy who was "thoroughly guilty," in a world in which "might and stupidity were constantly on the same side." It was an advantage that made Voltaire take as absolutes his own sociocultural prejudices: it gave him a supreme confidence in his own intelligence as well as a basic naïveté that made him assume it was possible to dominate one's language and put it in the service of a self-sufficient reason. The Voltairean perspective reduced the world to a zero degree of humanity, to a level of epistemological and ontological innocence; the class to which he belonged, the bourgeoisie, was so close to establishing its axiological hegemony that it could already refuse to believe in history and could posit "its own thought, its own common sense as a Nature that would be offended by any doctrine, by any intellectual system." For Barthes, Voltaire's reign over the domain of reason is a proprietorship whose legitimacy derives from its fundamental prerogative: the free play of intelligence is authorized by a closed system whose very existence is the proof of its validity. In this imaginary universe, a certain causality has been put in place by an original intelligence; within this system, there exists a limited possibility of freedom—it is the play that "the constructor of the machine allows for the movement of its parts. This play is Reason."[1]

Opposed to Voltaire stands the example of Jean-Jacques Rousseau, who represents the intellectual of good faith, fully conscious of a debilitating contradiction in his existence—a dilemma akin to that besetting today's critics. Beginning with Rousseau, according to Barthes, the intellectual will be "constantly thirsting for and wounded by a responsibility that he no longer will be able to either completely honor or completely evade, [and] will define himself by his bad conscience."[2] Such an intellectual is unable to claim the alibi of the Enlightenment because he realizes that his discourse can no longer draw its powers of conviction from an alleged objective force of its rationalism. Today's critic no longer aspires to the superior stance of the legislator or judge: for a writer, "true responsibility is to support literature as a failed commitment, as a Mosaic glance at the Promised Land of the real."[3] In a similar manner, from the perspective of a critic's position, "a true discourse is possible only when the responsibility of the interpreter toward the work is identifiable with the critic's responsibility toward his own discourse."[4] The critic's hope of legislating the world has been dashed by a reality that precludes any easy distinction of guilt and righteousness.

In retrospect, this brief and not very well known text of Roland Barthes can be seen as setting the tone and the terms of the whole structuralist debate around the legacy of the Enlightenment. For Barthes, what is noteworthy in Voltaire's approach is not the creative genius that epitomizes the spirit of the Enlightenment but a strategy. Thus we are told that "by associating all systems with Stupidity and all freedom of thought with Intelligence, Voltaire founded liberalism in its contradiction." By failing to raise the question of its own sociohistorical provenance, by discounting the reality of determinants to which its moral and intellectual authority could be attributed, liberalism could claim both moral and intellectual purity. This fundamental ideology of our modern age is therefore doubly deceitful; it is "evasive and wins on both counts, engaging in a perpetual alternation between bad faith and good conscience."[5]

The analysis of Voltaire's philosophy elaborated by Barthes is unorthodox, to say the least. Setting aside, for the time being, questions of fairness and accuracy (to which I turn in chapter 6) we can note that Barthes's characterization of Voltaire was certainly innovative. In this, Barthes was clearly situating his critique within the context of critical aims shared by the generation of French intellectuals that included the structuralists and the New Novelists. It was a generation of writers who were conscious of the radical importance of their creative and critical activities and who seriously intended to change society by subverting the traditional ways of thinking about literature. This claim was subject to several paradoxes, however, not the least of which was its lack of originality—something brought out by Barthes's discussion of Voltaire. Although Barthes locates the work of the structuralists in the context of the intellectual tradition inaugurated by Rousseau, his arguments point to a tradition that goes back even further and represents what could be considered one of the most characteristic and estimable aspects of French literature. I am referring to the tradition of the *moralistes*. I am also suggesting that current debates about the contributions or shortcomings of the structuralist enterprise can be explained in part by placing them within this tradition.

In the domain of French literary culture, the figure of the *moraliste* has a presence that has been consecrated by a long and most prestigious tradition. The lineage extends from Montaigne to Camus and includes such eminent representatives as Pascal, La Rochefoucauld, La Bruyère, Vauvenargues, Gide, and a number of others who—while not strictly identifiable by the designation of *moraliste*—have sufficiently manifested the concerns associated with the title to be designated honorary members of this select group: we could include Voltaire, Anatole France, Sartre, and even Céline. This is to say that the tradition of the *moraliste* is one that weighs heavily on the world of French letters—more heavily than is usually realized or acknowledged—and that the current intellectual debates and controversies are inevitably enmeshed in considerations that relate to this venerable and altogether French mode of thought.

Of course, the particular mix of the literary and the moral, of the intellectual and the ethical, varies with the individual thinker and has undergone a change in emphasis and approach since the time of Montaigne. The major contribution of the twentieth century in this regard has been to politicize the ethical component of this sort of philosophical reflection on human existence and behavior. In addition, the twentieth century introduced a specific form of debate centered on the intellectual's responsibilities. The debate was typically set off by an accusation of betrayal, and the title of Julien Benda's book—*La trahison des clercs*—published in 1927, has become a standard designation for this kind of indictment. Benda's purpose was to defend the prerogatives of rational thought and to argue that its function is to uphold the dignity of such universal notions as truth and justice over and above local, mundane, and—in particular—political concerns. Some thirty years later, Raymond Aron's *L'opium des intellectuels* made another epochal and lasting contribution to the debate. Aron viewed the domination of Marxism over the French intellectual world as a new type of betrayal and denounced the stifling limitations of this fashionable orthodoxy.

In the context of this traditional debate concerning the intellectual's obligations and responsibilities, the structuralist project has now become the newest example of the apparently cyclical *trahison des clercs*. The writers of the 1960s are accused of betraying modernity, of recklessly relativizing values, and of having set free the dark forces of nihilism and anarchism. The thought of the principal representatives of the structuralist period—Althusser, Lacan, Serres, Foucault, Veyne, Bourdieu, Derrida—has now been branded as the *pensée 68*.[6] This *pensée* is considered to have been both a cause and a symptom of the sociopolitical turmoil and cultural malaise that marked the events of 1968 in France; it is a way of thinking that, in some quarters, is held partly responsible for the political failure symptomized by these events and is still thought to hold a dangerous and deplorable sway over French philosophy.

Briefly, what is condemned is the irrationalism, anarchism, nihilism, promoted by the self-indulgent and esoteric theorizing of the *maîtres à penser* of the sixties. The common theme for which their works are denounced is an antihumanism that is said to threaten the very foundations of Western civilization. For Jacques Bouveresse, for example, the principal achievement of this philosophy has been to make Oswald Spengler's gloomy prophecy about the West's decline more credible because its net effect has been to bring about a unilateral moral disarmament that "would facilitate even more the task of the cleverest, strongest, and least scrupulous." Bouveresse subscribes to a thesis promulgated today by a number of German critics who see the structuralists of the sixties as engaged in an unfortunate rehearsal of Nietzschean themes—of the philosophical motifs that provided German fascism with the necessary intellectual prestige and justification. The sort of aggressive inventiveness that derives from pure speculation can only lead to disaster, warns Bouveresse: it is an approach that is strikingly exemplified by the central thesis of *Mein Kampf*.[7]

If on the one hand the "bashing" of the sixties in France could be attributed to a neoconservative trend, similar attacks directed against the *maîtres penseurs* have also come from a leftist orientation that saw structuralism as a strategy by which the bourgeoisie tried to resist the effects of Marxist critique. Thus Sartre shrugged off the enormous success of Foucault's *Les mots et les choses* by characterizing the book as "the latest barrier that the bourgeoisie has been able to erect against Marx."[8] Such an opinion appeared to be corroborated by subsequent developments. In light of the enthusiastic reception that structuralist theories enjoyed in the United States, certain writers were led to conclude that we live in an era characterized by the "apotheosis of the petite-bourgeoisie"; structuralist theories, naturally enough, found a congenial terrain in the United States—a country characterized by the author of a critical bestseller as "the promised land of contentless discourses." It seems that the foreign language departments of American universities, known for their "total lack of imagination," were only too happy to subscribe to the "hegemony of the signifier" because such a theoretical ploy was "the most likely pretense to touch the sensitivities of a people uncertain of its beginnings."[9]

Of course, such fanciful explanations tell us more about the quirkiness of the authors and certain aspects of the cultural climate in France than about the object of these analyses. From our side of the Atlantic, the story takes on an altogether different significance. When the structuralist theories were transplanted to the United States, they gained a new life but also acquired a cultural reality whose impact is still difficult to understand in all of its ramifications. The theories brought with them some of the stigma as well as the aura they had acquired in France, but they also found themselves transplanted to a cultural context that was, obviously, quite different. In the first place, whereas the political pretense of intellectual activism was laid to rest after 1968 in France, structuralist theories seemed to fit into the mood and purpose of intellectual activism of the sixties in this country. The poststructuralism that emerged and grew in the seventies blended quite readily with the remaining strains of a radical ethos by providing a theoretical framework for political activism.

There never was something called "poststructuralism" in France. Indeed, by the time the American importation of the works falling under this rubric was in full gear, the age of structuralism had drawn to a close there. However, it is also important to note that, while the prefix *post* did seem to imply at one time that structuralist theory had been somehow superseded, it is really impossible to make a clear distinction between structuralism and poststructuralism in the American context.[10] Even in France, the period of structuralist ascendancy is not so clear-cut as is generally supposed. In 1981 the magazine *Lire* conducted a survey asking some six hundred French intellectuals—writers, professors, artists, journalists, politicians—to name three living French thinkers whose work was still exerting the greatest influence on the "evolution of ideas, letters, arts, sciences, etc." The survey yielded a list of thirty-six names that included the cartoonist Claire Brétecher and the movie director Jean-Luc Godard. At the head of the list, and far ahead of the pack were three names: Claude Lévi-Strauss, Raymond Aron, and Michel Foucault; Jacques Lacan, was fourth and Simone de Beauvoir fifth; one notable absence—Jacques Derrida.[11]

What confuses the issue even more is that poststructuralism tends to be assimilated to deconstruction, a critical mode that has enjoyed a following in the United States it never had in France—one that is frequently considered, especially by enemies of theory, as a representative example of French theorizing. Thus, what has happened to deconstruction can be taken as an instructive sampling of the critical attitudes toward poststructuralism in general. Deconstruction has typically been attacked on at least two, contradictory accounts: "For American reviewers, deconstruction manages to be at once scandalous and too conservative."[12] On the one hand, deconstruction is attacked as a new sort of aestheticism that only serves the defenders of the status quo by giving an appearance of radicalness to an activity that has no real critical or political effectiveness. Deconstruction is also seen as a dogmatism which, while purporting to undermine the logocentric assumptions of Western culture, only succeeds in invalidating the theoretical ground of any critical position that is not couched in deconstructionist terms. The net critical effect of deconstruction is thus seen as a gratuitous, ludic strategy that reduces everything to a play of signifiers, to a problem of textuality, or to a question of literature. It is viewed as an aesthetics parading as an ethics and its significance is therefore considered academic.

On the other hand, deconstruction has also been perceived as part of a larger threat posed by the new theoretical and critical approaches to the established system of values. In this sense, an interesting parallel exists between the reaction in France and that in the United States: the sixties are also blamed in this country for having introduced anarchy and irresponsibility, especially on our campuses. Thus one critic traces the troubles besetting higher education today to the spirit of the sixties, a time when the university "willingly abandoned the one doctrine indispensable to its moral integrity—academic neutrality." What made the situation even worse in the following decade were the students admitted to graduate studies in particular; consequently, "the decline of the university in the last decade can be blamed on the 'second-rate intellects' who flocked to the graduate schools in·the 1970s." Some of these students eventually became professors and constitute today "a stratum of politicized educators bent on preparing the way for significantly left-oriented socioeconomic changes of the American polity."[13] Similar theses and accusations have subsequently produced books with such titles as *The Closing of the American Mind, The War against Intellect, Tenured Radicals,* and articles in the popular press with even more resounding claims: "America's College Campuses Are Now in Hands of Loony Left," trumpeted one recently.[14]

Among the critics who are the loudest and most persistent to blame radicals for having politicized campuses are political appointees such as William Bennett, onetime director of the National Endowment for the Humanities and former secretary of education, and Lynne Cheney, also a former director of NEH. The key to reclaiming the legacy of the humanities, according to Bennett, is to be found in good teaching, and a good teacher is "one who doesn't get involved in political issues"; consequently, "those interested in the humanities should be interested in more important things than Nicaragua."[15] One striking aspect of Bennett's campaign against the politicization of the campuses is his obliviousness to his own explicit political commitments. Thus, when Bennett traveled to

Stanford University to condemn the adoption of a core course entitled "Culture, Ideas, and Values" as being "primarily a political and not an educational decision," his action, obviously, "was in itself a political fact—indeed a fact of first importance. For a high official of the government to come to campus to pronounce judgment on a university's construction of its courses is an exercise of power at least as political as the campus demonstrations that the Secretary deplored as political."[16] One can only suppose that, for Cheney, Bennett, and other like-minded defenders of tradition, the promotion of Western civilization is by definition apolitical.

The attempt to segregate the cultural from the political appears particularly quixotic from a French perspective. A recent commentator on the French political scene points out that in France "artists and intellectuals are not perceived as kooks and weirdos or subverters of family values," but that politicians frequently try to enlist their aid and support:

> In France, artists and intellectuals have long felt close to the sources of political power. This has something to do with French history—a relationship between power and ideas formed as far back as the absolute monarchy of Louis XIV and his court at Versailles. It has something to do with the French educational system and the respect of ideas among French politicians—many of whom have been intellectuals themselves—and those who elect them. It has to do with the centralization of the country's cultural and political power in Paris, where everyone rubs shoulders with everyone else.[17]

Clearly, the vagueness and ambiguity of the term *political* are also responsible for the controversies and ensuing confusion that mark any consideration of the political involvement of intellectuals in this country. Moreover, attempts to sort out some of these issues are thwarted by "the persistent, and probably intentional, confusion between positions that may be described as intellectually radical, and those that are politically radical. Structuralists, semioticians, deconstructionists, psychocritics and the like were for many years attacked by the political left (especially Marxists and neo-Marxists) for the apparent lack of socially radical implications in their work."[18] Thus one of the principal causes of the misunderstanding is certainly linguistic, since the French have two terms, *le politique* and *la politique,* to designate a reality covered by only one word in English. The political implications of intellectual or literary activity are neither scandalous nor problematic in France because "the distinction between *le politique* and *la politique* has distant affinities with the distinction between *langue* and *parole, that is,* between language as a system and language as instantiated in speech."[19] *La politique* comprises the concrete manifestations and application of certain principles that derive from *le politique,* which is the symbolic matrix enveloping all social activity. It is this symbolic nature and origin of political thought that demands a complete reorientation in our understanding of the term *political* because "when we speak of symbolic organization, symbolic constitution, we seek to disclose beyond practices, beyond relations, beyond institutions which arise from factual givens, either natural or historical, an ensemble of articulations which are not *deducible* from nature or from history, but which order the apprehension of that which presents itself as real."[20] *Le politique* is thus no longer seen as the realm of a purposeful, instrumental application of a previously constituted knowledge but as a cultural subconscious patterning our knowledge of society and social relations.

In one sense, such an approach reveals a markedly Nietzschean predilection that a number of critics view as a deplorable tendency in contemporary French culture. It is based on the idea "that the image of a reality established rationally on a foundation (the image in which metaphysics has always represented the world) is but a 'reassuring' myth, well suited to a still primitive and barbaric humanity."[21] But this approach also fits in a cultural and intellectual tradition that takes for granted the conjunction of politics and literature, an alliance made evident by the practice of the *moralistes.* What was too often forgotten at the time when structuralism was brought to these shores was that the structuralists—as intellectuals—saw themselves irremediably committed to a political and ethical position. And although structuralist writings were frequently (explicitly or implicitly) meant to contradict or go beyond Marxist theory, they were still profoundly imbued with an ideology of the left. An issue of *La Quinzaine littéraire* reminds us of this peculiar aspect of French intellectual life: there are historical and cultural circumstances that place intellectuals in opposition to the established bourgeois morality and socioeconomic order. In a sense, it is the intellectual's function and prerogative to question the

scheme linking this morality to this order, and it is his or her professional obligation to reveal the self-serving interests that strive to
give this order a moral facade. As the editor of *La Quinzaine
littéraire* notes, there is no such thing as an intellectual of the right,
"because the foremost concern of the Right, in all countries, in all
circumstances, has been, continues to be to impose censorship, to
gag, to interdict thought."[22]

Although it manifests a negative, anarchistic, and even destruc-
tive approach to culture and values, this attitude of the left does not
deny the validity of the fundamental principles of democracy, freedom, and equality—on the contrary: "In France and elsewhere,
from 1830 to the present, an adherence to the left in the modern
sense, that is socialism, comes from the conviction that this movement incarnated the democratic, emancipatory, and egalitarian ideals of the French Revolution." Because these ideals were betrayed
by the bourgeoisie, which, from the time of the July Monarchy to
the regime of Pétain has consistently sided with antidemocratic and
antirepublican forces, French intellectuals have seen the coexistence
of social and cultural values in the context of the realm of quantita-
tive values of exchange promoted by capitalism as a flagrant contradiction: "It follows that between the intellectual and capitalism
there is frequently (not always, obviously) an antipathy in the
ancient—alchemic—sense of the word: 'a lack of affinity between
two substances.' "[23] The evolution of structuralism was obviously
inscribed within the framework of this antipathy; consequently,
from a structuralist perspective, the rhetoric of a liberal ideology
inherited from the Enlightenment could only be seen as an alibi.

It is this propensity for revealing collusions between systems of
power and cultural modes of representation that coalesced quite
naturally with the radical activism spawned by the concerns of the
sixties. One of the major contributions of structuralist theory is the
distrust it has inspired toward all forms of official cultural or ideological representation. Whatever seems natural and presents itself
as something inherent is to be viewed as a pretense—in the original
Latin sense of *praetendere,* a term referring to the action of drawing a
curtain in front of a stage. What the poststructuralists taught were
different strategies for finding out what lies behind the curtain and
the reasons for the curtain being drawn. They also showed that
there is no necessary relation or logical cause-effect link between

the pretense and the actual scene on the stage and that rule over one does not imply control of the other. For everything said and done there resonates an unsaid that is more fundamental, more consequential; on an individual level, our very being is dependent on an otherness that evades comprehension and control; on a social level, a principle of noncorrespondence marks the relation between the image a society creates of itself, for itself, and the actual mechanisms of the underlying sociopolitical strategies.

The traditional approach had been to reconcile the two dimensions of psychic and social activity by covering up discrepancies between the two with explanatory paradigms that negate as much as possible the unknowable, uncontrollable, and unpredictable. Poststructuralists inspired a general skepticism with regard to all such procedures of rationalization and initiated a reversal in the strategies of intellect.[24] Thus, instead of starting with a systematic explanation within which to incorporate the observable, they begin with a description or retelling of the observed that makes the observer an integral part of the investigation. Because the privilege of the norm, of the rational, of the "fully human" is ratified by "objective" knowledge, a deconstruction of this procedure can be accomplished by erecting an antiknowledge that is aware of all that is excluded; by disclosing the preponderance of unreason over reason and the insistent presence of the void surrounding reason's alleged self-sufficiency. Derrida reminds us that " 'thought' requires *both* the principle of reason *and* what is beyond the principle of reason, the *arkhe* and an-archy."[25] Thought is not true to itself if it does not include the metaphysical question of being, if it fails to consider the abyss over which rationality has constructed its systems of coherence. Consequently, it has to be recognized that "the principle of reason installs its empire only to the extent that the abyssal question of the being that is hiding within it remains hidden, and with it the question of the grounding of the ground itself."[26] This truth of thought is therefore to be situated in the Other and any truth-claims made in the name of reason—any subjects of reason—are to be brought into question in terms of the fundamental lack at the heart of any subject. To cover up this lack, to bridge this abyss, discourses and pacts are made, reasons given, and the reality of subjects is constituted. It is but a makeshift reality, as the structuralists saw it, the fabric that makes up the human drama. It was clear to them that "what constitutes the background of all human drama, of all theatrical drama in particular, is the existence of established bonds, knots, pacts. Human beings are already linked to one another by commitments that have determined their place, their name, their essence. Then, other discourses come along, other commitments, other words. It is certain that at some points it is then necessary to unravel the ties."[27]

This metaphysical question of being, the void of the abyss that founds rationality, becomes thus a justification for critical activism and a principle of political involvement. In this sense, structuralist discourse made it seem possible to unravel the ties binding and defining subjects and strove to open up the possibility for different commitments and different arrangements for governing the relations that link humans. It is also in this sense that the work of structuralists was inescapably political, as Derrida pointed out: "It is impossible, now more than ever, to dissociate the work we do, within one discipline or several, from a reflection on the political and institutional conditions of that work. Such a reflection is unavoidable. It is no longer an *external* complement to teaching and research; it must make its way through the very objects we work with, shaping them as it goes, along with our norms, procedures, and aims. We cannot not speak of such things."[28] Such a definition of the political has of course seemed inordinately tame to critics still imbued with the traditional notions of critical activism derived from an Enlightenment ethos. From a structuralist perspective, it was this very ethos that was to be questioned, and what structuralist theory sought to demonstrate before all else was the inadmissibility of any strategy derived from the unexamined authority of the subject.

CHAPTER 2

FROM THE *COGITO* TO THE SUBJECT

SKEPTICISM ABOUT CLAIMS to impose the law of reason on human affairs hardly originated with the structuralists: they were simply taking farther than anyone else the implications of a process that had begun much earlier, one that culminates today in what could be called the era of postmodern disenchantment. The skeptical strain in Western thinking can indeed be considered an integral part of modernity's evolution. Starobinski, for example, opposes the thought of Montaigne to that of Descartes and locates the two thinkers at a major bifurcation in Western thought: the Cartesian path, which was to lead to a conceptual sacralization of the future at the end of the eighteenth century, also took Western civilization to what Starobinski calls the "modern attitude: extrapolating from the example of science and technology, where results are predictable, man has developed a fondness for the idea that he can *shape* his own destiny." Not surprisingly, such a presumption regarding the power of true knowledge has taken us to the ultimate illusion, which is "the belief that one has escaped illusion, that one has come close to the truth of being, that one has found the way to weed out falsehood and error. More precisely, the illusion consists in the belief that one has moved beyond the uncertain realm of ethical decision and into the realm where certain knowledge can be infallibly applied."[1] What strikes a postmodern perception of this cognitive process is its circularity, which appears thus as a fundamental flaw canceling any claim to know. The mechanism on which Western ways of knowing and authorizing knowledge about the world and "man" have been founded is no longer able to function because its strategy has been disclosed.

The critique of the subject, that is, the questioning and eventual invalidation of the principle of a self-assured and self-sufficient source of thought, is arguably the most important legacy of the so-called structuralist movement:

> The full thrust of the structuralist enterprise, as Foucault and other post-structuralists have granted repeatedly, devolves from suspending the *privilege* of the perceiving subject—that is, the I, the ego, the source, eventually the author—that seizes the phenomenal world as present to consciousness. The structuralist argument holds that the perception, the grasping, the apprehension of the phenomenal world, and similarly the constitution of the known world of scientific objects of knowledge, has to be construed in a much more complex way that does not privilege the subjective over the objective, the conscious over the unconscious, and so forth.[2]

Because the subject was central to structuralist theories, it can be seen as a unifying theme that, in retrospect, justifies the application of the label "structuralist" to what was a fairly disparate group of writers.[3] Instead of taking the subject to be the source of language and knowledge about the world, the structuralists construed it as a position registering perceptions in terms of a linguistic and cognitive aptitude it had assimilated without controlling it. The structuralists thereby gave their approach a fundamentally subversive potential because by attacking the subject they were invalidating the very foundations of Western philosophy. They were thus able to "criticize the assumption of much of modern thought that theoretical discourse is a direct expression of a truth in the theorist's mind, that this truth in some way captures historical reality, and that the question of freedom entails the appropriation of this truth by historical agents and their subsequent action to actualize it."[4] They were also calling our attention to the need to critically re-evaluate the history of the truths that have constituted the Western sense of cultural, social, and political identity; by calling attention to the contingent nature of the subject that was at the core of modernity's sense of self-worth, they were, in effect, proclaiming the end of an era.

It is, of course, possible to view the same history differently and to argue for the continued validity of the Western subject. One recent and powerful statement defending the viability and continued relevance of modernity's axiological paradigm is found in the magisterial study by Charles Taylor, *Sources of the Self: The Making of the Modern Identity.* Taylor, like the structuralists, also recognizes that the modern subject is undergoing a crisis; however, his diagnosis of the crisis, as well as his analysis of the history leading up to it, is clearly motivated by a desire to restore the patient's former health and vigor. For Taylor the subject is undergoing a crisis because it has been set free of its ethical moorings. Taylor's purpose is thus twofold: he intends to reveal the inescapably moral dimension of Western notions of selfhood and to argue that this self owes its identity to sources it cannot renounce with impunity. Taylor informs us that "the intention of this work was one of retrieval, an attempt to uncover buried goods through rearticulation—and thereby to make these sources again empower, to bring the air back again into the half-collapsed lungs of the spirit."[5] These "goods" are the various influences that account for Western forms of self-reflexivity, self-exploration, and self-control; they are the philosophical sources that articulate our moral and spiritual intuition and guide our lives. The facets of the Western self are multiple and varied and can be traced back to such diverse thinkers as Augustine, Descartes, Montaigne, and Kant; they derive both from the secular approach exemplified by Enlightenment naturalism and the religious affirmation of a Judeo-Christian tradition. It is this aggregate of "epistemological, metaphysical, and moral motives" that has given shape to a modern form of consciousness and "has fed our faith in ourselves as a reforming civilization, capable of reaching higher moral goals than any previous age has." Taylor also shows that all attempts at refuting the inherently moral identity of the Western subject have been deluded in one way or another because they have failed to recognize their own reliance on traditional ideals; moreover, the purely secular and antireligious thrust of such approaches has only succeeded in "stifling the response in us to some of the deepest and most powerful spiritual aspirations that humans have conceived."[6]

Taylor's appeal to "spiritual aspirations" clearly indicates that, for him, the list of goods is really meaningless without the greatest one of all: a good transcending the history of all the others, one that has always been there and that still informs the concept of the modern subject. This good, for Taylor, is revealed in the phenomenon of a "personal resonance" the individual achieves with the world, a resonance that is fully realized by accepting that "the sense of the superiority of the good life, and the inspiration to attain it, must come from the agent's sense of his own dignity as a rational being" and by understanding that "great as the power of naturalist sources might be, the potential of a certain theistic perspective is incomparably greater."[7] In the final analysis, then, while Taylor endows the modern individual's moral core with the lingering effects of a long historical tradition, his argument must rely on an act of faith to justify the ethical imperative that, for him, defines the essence of the Western subject. It is also the need to defend this faith that motivates and shapes his critique of those who have contributed most to the dismantling of this subject.

One of Taylor's goals is to undo the effects of what he calls the "neo-Nietzschean type of theory," an approach that, according to him, has ignored the fundamental commitment to "benevolence and justice" underlying the various philosophies of the subject. For Taylor, philosophies such as that of Foucault appear to have been "claiming . . . impossible neutrality, which recognized no claim as binding." He finds implausible a view that holds all intellectual and moral positions as equally justifiable because "the point of view from which we might constate that all orders are equally arbitrary, in particular that all moral views are equally so, is just not available to us humans."[8] The position Taylor attributes to Foucault and other like-minded thinkers is clearly a product of his critical tactic, which is to make the views of his opponents into a negative of his own. Taylor's argument, in this regard, is typical of the strategy used by those who attack the "relativism" of postmodern philosophers.

The neutrality alleged by Taylor is certainly not a position that Foucault or other "neo-Nietzscheans" have claimed to occupy. Far from arrogating an Olympian perspective on human affairs, Foucault makes the "personal resonance" of his real-life experiences the starting point of his investigations. Recognizing his own intimate involvement with the subjects of his analyses, Foucault came to believe that "the critical question today has to be turned back into a positive one: in what is given to us as universal, necessary, obligatory, what place is occupied by whatever is singular, contingent, and the product of arbitrary constraints?" The arbitrariness is not in our choice but in whatever imposes itself on us to mold our choices and attitudes: "This entails an obvious consequence: that criticism is no longer going to be practiced in the search for formal structures with universal value, but rather as a historical investigation into the events that have led us to constitute ourselves and to recognize ourselves as subjects of what we are doing, thinking, saying." The approach is therefore very much like that of Taylor—with one important difference: it will not seek to extol, revalidate, or re-legitimize processes that have constituted the subject but "will separate out, from the contingency that has made us what we are, the possibility of no longer being, doing, or thinking what we are, do, or think."[9] It is a matter of a fundamental difference in "personal resonances" toward the world. While Taylor is in awe of "the stupendous humanitarian efforts of the nineteenth and twentieth centuries,"[10] Foucault, as we will see in the next chapter, shares in the postmodern suspicion of all Western claims of progress and ethical superiority and manifests a fundamental mistrust of optimistic and admiring accounts of civilized achievement.

Foucault's recommendation was that we "listen to the victims, not to the theoreticians"; in this respect, he was less interested in registering and rationalizing achievements, in providing programs for further progress and emancipation, than in undoing the harm that had come from too great a reliance on the theories of system makers; as Michel Rybalka remarks pointedly, "Foucault is not the philosopher of liberation, but of counteralienation, he cannot conceive of better things to come, but he wants to repair, to alleviate the damage which is being done to others."[11] The lesson of Foucault's work can therefore serve as a defense against smugness; it offers an effective protection against what Kenneth Galbraith has characterized as "the power of contentment over belief," the lure of complacency threatening to entrap those who fail to take into account one of the more important lessons of history:

> The most nearly invariant is that individuals and communities that are favored in their economic, social and political condition attribute social virtue and political durability to that which they themselves enjoy. That attribution, in turn, is made to apply even in the face of commanding evidence to the contrary. The beliefs of the fortunate

are brought to serve the cause of continuing contentment, and the economic and political ideas of the time are similarly accommodated. There is an eager political market for that which pleases and reassures.[12]

The poststructuralists belong to a generation that has not found the evidence of civilized achievement very impressive. Foucault, for one, was struck by the discrepancy between the optimism implicit in a humanistic interpretation of culture and his own experience. Moreover, he was aware that the discrepancy was not due simply to a personal obsession but was symptomatic of an entire era. This awareness led him to reflect on the discursive strategies that function to minimize, naturalize, or cover up such discrepancies. The earliest and arguably the most effective cover-up was precisely the tactic making possible the emergence of the modern subject—the *cogito.*

Taylor is of course quite justified when he singles out Nietzsche's influence as the most detrimental for the modern subject. As Sarah Kofman has shown, Nietzsche dealt a devastating blow to the viability of the Cartesian model by disclosing the fundamental flaw undermining the *cogito.* He showed that Descartes's tactic was successful only because it was able to ignore its own leap of faith, which was its reliance on grammar. This faith in grammar "made him neglect to give enough attention to language to perceive that reason itself was simply one of its categories."[13] Nietzsche pointed out that what Descartes's famous assertion demonstrated above all was a belief in logic—in the connecting power of *ergo;* it also showed a complete lack of concern for the highly problematic status of the two other terms, because "one would have to know what 'being' is in order to get the *sum* from the *cogito;* one would also have to know what 'knowing' is: one starts from belief in logic—in the *ergo* before all else—and not uniquely from the position of a fact! Is 'certainty' possible in knowledge? Isn't immediate certainty perhaps a *contradictio in adjecto?* What is knowing in relation to being? For whoever brings to all these points a ready-made belief, Cartesian prudence no longer has meaning; it comes too late."[14] The Cartesian formula does not demonstrate the necessity of its conclusion, only the necessity of a belief in a subject, in identity; it is therefore a veritable article of faith. But, Kofman argues, "faith, in fact, leads in all cases to stupidity. . . . Any long-standing belief eventually *becomes* stupid; which amounts to saying, in the precise language of our modern psychologists, that its motives sink 'into the unconscious'—they disappear into it."[15] The object of criticism in the Nietzschean lineage has been to recover what has been forgotten for having been covered up or repressed.

One of the more recent and thorough critical investigations elaborating further the Nietzschean critical approach is to be found in the work of the philosopher Michel Meyer. Meyer finds that the currently perceived crisis in Western humanism is attributable to the discovery of a whole dimension of a priori assumptions and metaphysical commitments that had been lying dormant under the evidence of the *cogito*. He argues, for example, that the method and the metaphysical presuppositions are intractably locked in a circular pattern of mutual support. The circularity of the famous method manifests itself in several ways. While Descartes begins by submitting everything to a radical doubt, the doubting turns out to be rhetorical as soon as it becomes clear that its purpose is really to produce the first certainty in Descartes's chain of evidences: the assertion that to doubt is to think. Descartes's doubt is already infused with an a priori certitude and is enunciated only because it has from the outset the propensity for canceling itself out. In a similar fashion, Descartes's procedure for establishing the certainty of his existence is predicated on a question that already holds the answer: "The question of knowing if I am is already decided by that of knowing if I think, whereas the one is expected to establish the other. . . . How could I doubt that I am, if I doubt? The answer is indeed already in the question, which is nothing more than the rhetorical form of the statement '*I think.*'"[16] Not only is Descartes's procedure inherently tautological but it achieves its ends by ignoring the steps through which certainty is reached as well as the initial condition of freedom that the procedure implies; what is obvious to Descartes can be dissected in a number of incremental assumptions that are all subsumed under the leap of faith leading from an initial doubt to the *cogito*. According to Peter Schouls, "Unless we reach the *cogito* we cannot hope to validate reason. Unless we can validate reason we cannot accept as trustworthy anything which reason presents to the mind. Lacking both of these, we cannot make progress in the pursuit of truth. But, as Descartes makes abundantly clear, we cannot reach the *cogito* unless we suspend judgment and unless we use method. Both activities involve acts of freedom. The freedom involved in acts like these, one must conclude, plays for Descartes a role more fundamental than that of the *cogito*."[17]

Descartes's difficulties, according to Meyer, stem from the necessity to devise a strategy that can operate only in terms of two languages—one to be validated and another with which to validate; obviously, they are one and the same, and the *Logos* Descartes wishes to found is the one he relies on from the outset. Likewise, the derivation of a certitude of being from an awareness of thinking is a foregone conclusion because the self is the *I* already present in the *cogito;* the full and self-conscious weight of the subject is there at the moment of the enunciation, since Descartes's *cogito* "posits as existing that which is deduced *a priori* when it is this existence that is precisely in question." Lastly, Meyer points out that Descartes's formulation of the relation of thought to being is not logical: it is not because "I think" that "I am"; at most, it could be said that "I am a being that thinks" because "one cannot jump from 'I think' to 'I am' but only to 'I am thinking.' "[18] The truth of the subject's existence, the evidence of being, is hardly a consequence of thought; it is there at the outset.

What Descartes accomplishes, in effect, is a leap from the realm of empirical, positivistic evidence to that of transcendental and metaphysical themes. Descartes's strategy is thus subject to a curious paradox: it is self-contradictory and self-invalidating precisely because it claims to be logical and self-validating. As Meyer shows, the method is partly intuitive, partly deductive. On the one hand, intuition is "the irrational part of absolute reason, thus its very impossibility." On the other, deduction works only because "it arranges an already constituted knowledge." Not surprisingly, Descartes has to have recourse to God, who will guarantee the truthfulness of thought. Only this reassuring premise ensures that the subject will find itself established as self-sufficient, autonomous, and unquestionable in its essence.

In retrospect then, two things appear remarkable about Descartes's procedure: its duplicitous strategy and its success. What is also striking is the tenacity of a paradigm that appears so flimsy today; indeed, the evidence of *cogito*'s disintegration is all around us and has been noticeable for some time: "It is the fracturing of ancient harmonies, in music as in painting, both more 'abstract' than ever. It is the formal break in poetry, with Mallarmé, Eliot or Pound. It is the problematisation of prose itself, through the decentering of a narrative without beginning or end, without a totalizing subject, something the New Novel has effectively illustrated; but it is also the enigma becoming itself an object of fiction, as in Kafka."[19] What literature, art, and music have demonstrated is the fallacy at the center of Descartes's project—the failure to appreciate the constitutive power of words in the formation of ideas. Thinking reality was directly available via the medium of language, Descartes "confused the fictive unity of the word with the simplicity of the clear and distinct idea, the simple with the complex." Thus, his "naïveté is to have believed that he could 'think' without language, that he could 'rid himself' of language in favor of reason, at the very moment he was obeying the unsurpassable constraints of language, at the very moment he was interpreting things according to a schema inherent to language—a schema belonging not to a pure mind but indispensable to a living man determined to appropriate the world and affirm his power."[20]

We may well wonder then why Descartes was so eager to establish grounds for certitude and why he was so readily trapped in his rush to demonstrate the truth of his being. Nietzsche shows that the trap was unavoidable, "for to believe in reason, cause, effect, the subject and the predicate, to believe in all these grammatical categories inherent to language, is the very essence of metaphysical thought, of thought itself."[21] For Nietzsche, the naïveté is directly attributable to a desire to appropriate; Descartes's purpose was to "grasp," and, as Kofman explains it, "this is the activity inherent in the will to power that is formative of the concept (*Begriff*). The etymology of the word is symptomatic of the brutality of this mastering project and reveals the illusion of a pure, innate, a priori idea, of an eternally 'simple' truth, sheltered from historical violence." The guiding principle for Descartes in his quest for clear and indubitable truths was simplicity, "the red-iron brand of the concept that suppresses differences and singularities—a change to the benefit of an empty abstraction that disfigures reality and that is in the service of the allied forces of morality and religion."[22] The pattern was thus set: the workings of society were thenceforth made amenable to the explanatory and legitimating capacity of abstractions that were to constitute the metaphysics of modernity.

At the center of this metaphysics was the subject, which, as we saw, became the principal concern of structuralist and poststructuralist critique. In the wake of this criticism, the nature of truths about the subject changed from self-evident to contingent and aporetic. The project to investigate the cultural, historical, and epistemological substratum supporting the subject relegated conscious thought to a secondary, derivative level of importance; consciousness came to represent a small part of the psychic reality of a subject and lost the determining and controlling prerogatives it had enjoyed in modernity's humanistic way of interpreting psychic reality:

> Conscious thought, then, must be seen as the "overdetermined" manifestation of a multiplicity of structures that intersect to produce that unstable constellation the liberal humanists call the "self." These structures encompass not only unconscious sexual desires, fears and phobias, but also a host of conflicting material, social, political and ideological factors of which we are equally unaware. It is this highly complex network of conflicting structures, the anti-humanist would argue, that produces the subject and its experiences, rather than the other way round.[23]

This strategy of a reversal gave structuralism its potential for effectuating a deconstruction of the familiar networks of knowledge and power, of the culturally ingrained beliefs sustaining the subject's claims to effective and autonomous agency.

It is without doubt the work of Jacques Lacan that called for the most radical reorientation in our thinking about the subject by bringing out the paradoxical complexity of our involvement with language and with others. The first and perhaps most important consequence of Lacan's investigations was the realization that the identity of the "I" that stands for the subject is nothing one can put a finger on—it is not an entity, it is neither stable nor tangible. Moreover, identity is not even conceivable prior to the subject's encounter with others, before it engages in an intersubjective exchange with others. It is in coming into contact with others that the subject comes into being—first as a mirror image, when it sees itself reflected in the eyes and the attitudes of others; then, as it learns to speak, it forms a more self-assertive identity by entering and becoming a participant in the symbolic field of language. However, by opening up the dimension of the unconscious, language only aggravates the split in the subject because "the unconscious permits the internalization of something that remains resolutely outside the subject—the symbolic function of language."[24] An unbridgeable gap is thus created between the subject's experience of selfhood and what it can say about itself: "Language does not just establish a bond, but also reveals the fundamental inadequacy of the subject to its own truth, its incapacity to realize the complete resonance of the symbolic and social systems within which it moves."[25]

The individual is thus aware from the moment of his or her entry into relationships with others that dependency is the defining principle of life. Because the subject knows its identity to be constituted by others and its meaning given by a symbolic dimension over which it has no control, it knows it is incomplete and becomes alienated from itself. At the same time, the subject is also driven by an irresistible urge to compensate for the lack at the core of its very being; it is moved by a desire that becomes the driving force motivating the individual's life: "Desire is, for Lacan, the fundamental defining trait of human existence. It is the element that renders inadequate any strictly perceptual or cognitive model of a subject, which is from its origin intersubjective and unconscious."[26] To satisfy this desire—which is also a "desire of the Other," a desire for the desire of the other—the subject seeks the recognition that is gained in intersubjective encounters. This meaning or truth is produced in the exchanges in which it engages, but since truth always resides outside the subject, it escapes the subject's control and is ceaselessly reconstituted. The quest is endless, therefore, and the subject is forever prevented from attaining the truth of its being. The truth of the subject, Lacan shows, resides in the Other, which is "the place where the I who speaks constitutes itself with the one who hears."[27] Moreover, "there is no Other of the Other," there is no metalanguage that can say what is true about what language says, "since truth founds itself in that it speaks, and that it has no other means for doing this."[28] At the same time, inadequate as it is, communication with others offers the only means of pursuing the quest of desire and imposes therefore an ethical obligation. It forces us to recognize that as we seek to address the Other, we cannot do it on our own, we can only do it through others who are equally situated with regard to the lack in their being: "This discourse of the other is not the discourse of the abstract other, of the other in the dyad, of my correspondent, not even of my slave; it is the discourse of the circuit in which I am integrated."[29] Our subjectivity gains its meaning from an interaction with others because "the subject is always subject to the Symbolic order." It is no more than "a locus of relations, a point of intersection."[30] Consequently, we incur an ethical debt owed to all other subjects whose participation constitutes the chain of significations we call a society.

On his first visit to the United States, on the occasion of the colloquium on structuralism held at Johns Hopkins, Lacan illustrated this notion of the subject, as well as the ambiguities it involved with the story of a personal experience. It was an anecdote concerning some difficulties he had had in rearranging furniture in his hotel room in Baltimore. Having told his story, Lacan posed the question of *its* subject: "What sort of subject characterizes a style of society in which everyone is theoretically as ready to help you as the question 'May I help you?' . . . implies? . . . What is the nature of this subject, then, which is based on this first principle, and which, on the other hand, makes it impossible to get service?" These questions had occurred to Lacan as he watched the performance of the task he had requested. At first, he had had trouble finding the person authorized to provide the service he required. Nevertheless, after several attempts, Lacan tells us, "I got the housekeeper and was then entitled to the service of two blacks. They arrived and, apparently paying very little attention to my request (they even seemed to be listening to something else), they did what I asked. They did it, I would say, *almost* perfectly, for there remained a few little imperfections in the job, but such definite imperfections that they could not have been unintentional."[31]

It is at this juncture that Lacan locates the question of the subject, "on the level of this *gap*—which does not fit into *intra* or *inter* or *extra* subjectivity." The question concerns, then, the gap separating the theoretical, ritual, offer of service from its practical realization. It is a question of a discrepancy that opposes what is supposed to take place to what is evident, that contrasts the ritualized theoretical representation of social interaction to the observable social reality. For Lacan, this gap stands for the alienating effect of racial discrimination inherent in American culture. It is also in this context that the behavior of the two blacks acquires its full significance: they behave as if they were not listening because, after all, this world of the whites with their courtesy and the principle of the "May I help you" does not really concern them. During the course of their existence, they have become well aware of the symbolic pact, of the fundamental law that determines their place in society—a racist law that is in flagrant contrast with the official slogans of equality, democracy, concern for the welfare of all. Their body language is an expression of their awareness that they are not fully integrated in the symbolic circuit; white society keeps them from entering the Other and limits their status to that of imaginary constructs whose partial existence is determined by the superficial distinction of their color: "It is when the subject endeavors to invoke another subject in its totality that that other becomes Other, for it succeeds in passing beyond its partial and imaginary determination of that other."[32] Racism is thus the subject of the story, it is what determines the reality of subject for the two black men in question, what defines their situation as subjects at the intersection of the imaginary and symbolic orders.

The subject of racism comes up again, some twenty years later, in an interview Lacan gave to Jacques-Alain Miller on French television. To Miller's question—"What gives you the confidence to prophesy the rise of racism? And why the devil do you have to speak of it?"—Lacan simply replies, "Because it doesn't strike me as funny and yet, it's true." He then provides an explanation couched in his characteristically abstruse manner of expressing a reality that resists representation and explaining: "With our *jouissance* going off the track, only the Other is able to mark its position, but only insofar as we are separated from this Other. Whence certain fantasies—unheard of before the melting pot." We have here the familiar theme of the "desire of the Other" played out in all its ambiguity as a "desire for the desire of the other." The existence of the Other is fed by fantasms—by the imaginary of themes of a moral and cultural superiority derived from the fact of a very real economic superiority. Thus the desire of the other becomes that of the "underdeveloped," of the people of color, the inhabitants of the Third World; this desire is the envious admiration inhabitants of the developed nations attribute to the other. It is an envy that valorizes our advantage and our prosperity and provides a gratification all the more libidinal because there are others who are deprived, who are excluded from our world of conspicuous consumption. The truth of this paradox is both banal and striking: there is no "development" without a corresponding "underdevelopment." The developed cannot exist, let alone enjoy life, without the underdeveloped; moreover, they have to create ties of dependence, they have to make the underdeveloped a product of their own development: "Leaving this other to his own mode of *jouissance,* that would only be possible by not imposing our own on him, by not thinking of him as underdeveloped."[33]

The pretense of humanistic, civilizing, and humanitarian discourses that Western nations have promoted for expanding the reach of their colonizing projects is maintained in place by an unrestrained narcissism and hedonism: "Given, too, the precariousness of our own mode, which from now on takes its bearings from the ideal of an overcoming [*plus de jouir*], which is, in fact, no longer expressed in any other way, how can one hope that the empty forms of humanhysterianism [*humanitairerie*] disguising our extortions can continue to last?" Lacan therefore foresees the inevitable rise of conservatism accompanied by a renewal of religious fervor, two developments that will only serve to shore up the forces of oppression and exploitation: "Even if God, thus newly strengthened, should end up ex-sisting, this bodes nothing better than a return to his baneful past."[34] The subject of Western culture is thus to be located in this gap between the symbolic force of desire exacerbated by the imaginary promotion of consumption and a material existence legitimized by an unholy alliance of humanitarian, nationalistic, and religious themes. It is at this juncture that individuals gain an identity processed by the system, an identity created to serve the ends of that system.

For the structuralists, it was an identity to be resisted, and their project consisted in devising new modes of conceiving and construing the subject. While Lacan did most to reveal the complexities of the psyche that entered in the creation and maintenance of the human subject, Michel Foucault was interested in the historical reality of the different modes in which subjects have been and continue to be constituted. At the same time, Foucault shared with Lacan a fascination with the vast expanse of unchartered territory that had been revealed through the gap the *cogito* used to cover.

CHAPTER 3

BETWEEN IDENTITY AND THE OTHER: THE SUBJECT OF MICHEL FOUCAULT

THE STRUCTURALISTS DERIVED many of their insights from the realization that we are not free to make the choices we make, that we are tied to discourses, pacts, unwritten agreements that determine what we think and how we act and that the ideal of free inquiry was a utopian aspiration at best. It was in this manner that they overturned most radically the fundamental understanding of which Western thought constructed its self-assertiveness, a self-confidence it gained by positing an original freedom enabling thought to found itself.

While Foucault rejected the label of structuralist, he did recognize an essential point of convergence in the work of the principal representatives of the so-called structuralist period. He noted a basic similarity between his own approach and those of Althusser and Lacan, for example, because the crucial problem for all of them was, he believed, "a matter of calling this theme of the subject into question once again, that great, fundamental postulate which French philosophy, from Descartes until our own time, had never abandoned."[1] In the work of Foucault himself, this concern becomes a matter of analyzing the constraints and limits the Cartesian model had imposed on thought. This approach, in turn, brings with it "an obvious consequence: that criticism is no longer going to be practiced in the search for formal structures with universal value, but rather as a historical investigation into the events that have led us to constitute ourselves as subjects of what we are doing, thinking, saying."[2] In this regard, we can see Foucault situating his inquiry in the hermeneutic tradition inaugurated by Montaigne:

"The experience of interpretation, as Montaigne's text insinuates, founds itself on the recognition that language, in a general and systematic fashion, and individual acts of interpretation, in particular, generate the conditions and limits of and for the possibility of understanding." We can also note that Foucault's hermeneutic strategy adopts a dual movement comparable to the tactic of Montaigne, whose writing also proceeds "by way of a *commentary* that turns away from itself, toward a different text, *and* that turns in on itself."[3] Thus, for Foucault, the project of deconstructing the subject is made possible by the understanding that a genealogical critique requires a dual orientation: a critical examination of modernity cannot proceed without developing a parallel inquiry into the critic's own role and prerogatives. The subject of criticism is inescapably double because it is both source and object. Indeed, it is the object of critique *because* it is at the same time its source. For Foucault, then, the act of criticism becomes also a matter of deconstructing his own identity.

This paradoxical aspect of the subject finds itself replicated in the specific case of identity. The paradox is the following: identity is what is naturally given and is therefore considered as a possession, yet it is also that which possesses the individual. If, on the one hand, identity is constituted by a personal experience and an individual history, it is also and inevitably a product of the otherness of cultural, social, and linguistic determinants. As the individual reconstructs and reflects upon an imaginary identity, he or she cultivates an illusion of conscious control that only serves to occlude the aleatory and contingent nature of this imaginary essence. Thus, in a sense, identity is our metaphysical refuge, it is the pretense serving to link our history and History, our self-conscious and purposeful use of language to the Logos that makes our speech possible. It is an explanatory system that reconciles our self-image with our being, one that also has the virtue of placing other humans within the context of a fundamental nature, a teleological design, or a scientific paradigm.

To escape the metaphysical trap, to avoid this confusion between thought and being, between language and essence, Foucault finds it important to stress that the subject "is not a substance; it is a form and this form is not above all or always identical to itself." Thus, an individual enacts different forms of relationship with one's self depending on the particular situation—political or sexual, for example—in which the subject is called to function. In each case, the subject's function is determined by the dictates of a particular code: "It is precisely the historical constitution of these different forms of subject relating to games of truth that interests me."[4] Foucault's own relation to the discursive dimension that gives shape to his thought thus becomes a central and constitutive component of his investigations.

It is also a highly ambiguous relationship since Foucault seeks to break or escape a dependency he finds unavoidable. Consequently, the purpose of the genealogical critique he elaborates is to "separate out, from the contingency that has made us what we are, the possibility of no longer being, doing, or thinking what we are, do, or think."[5] This critical purpose constitutes a basic component of Foucault's intellectual strategy: we write, he says, "to be other than what we are."[6] Consequently, the intellectual curiosity that motivates his archaeological and genealogical pursuits is "not the curiosity that seeks to assimilate what it is proper for one to know, but that which enables one to get free of oneself [se déprendre de soi-même]." The purpose of writing is therefore to "know to what extent the exercise of thinking one's own history can free thought from what it thinks silently and to allow it to think otherwise."[7]

The motif of *penser autrement* is of course a familiar one in Foucault's work and is to be found there from the earliest publications. It is most explicit when Foucault speaks of himself and his writing. His characterization of his own subjectivity expresses a dichotomy due to the realization that "to speak is to do something—something other than to express what one thinks, to translate what one knows."[8] On the other hand, Foucault also acknowledges the massive indoctrination to which, he realizes, he has been subjected. The metaphorical expressiveness of such statements as "I have been bottle-fed with knowledge" and "I have muddled about in knowledge" suggests the keenness of Foucault's self-consciousness with regard to the educational and cultural nurturing he underwent.[9] This awareness brings with it the inescapable corollary, which is a rejection of an identity derived from this culture and education. The rejection is all the more pronounced because such an identity is closely bound to the notion of essence, of being, and is consequently to be considered a product of the epistemological configuration that gave rise to the figure of "man" at the beginning of the nineteenth century. Identity is therefore inextricably enmeshed in political strategies and involved with the power-knowledge effects applied by discourse.

Fortunately, because this identity is a form and not an essence, it is not unalterable. What creates the possibility of escape or transformation is a disjuncture that exists between the dimension shaping our knowledge of the world and our experience of the world. For Foucault, this knowledge and this experience constitute different levels of our apprehension of reality. It is by juxtaposing these two levels in the act of writing that the possibility of transforming the subject is realized: by writing exploratory books that attempt to recover the historical truth of certain modes of subjection, Foucault aims at having not only "an experience of what we are today" but also, and more importantly, "an experience that might permit an alteration, a transformation, of the relationship we have with ourselves and our cultural universe: in a word, with our knowledge (*savoir*)."[10] This procedure is a "game of truth and fiction" or, as Foucault also refers to it, of "evidence and fabrication." Foucault recognizes that, although he bases his books on "true" documents, they are no more than artful constructs, that is, fictions. Nevertheless, they can be quite effective because the experience of confronting the evidence of the past with what passes for truth in the present "will permit us to see clearly what links us to our modernity and at the same time will make it appear modified to us. This experience . . . permits us to single out certain mechanisms (for example, imprisonment, penalization, etc.) and at the same time to separate ourselves from them by perceiving them in a totally different form."[11]

Truth, as Foucault has shown, is ultimately political in nature and is predicated on knowledge-power strategies operative in a given society and age. Truth in this regard has not set humans free but has instituted subjection, since "the man described for us, whom we are invited to free, is already in himself the effect of a subjection much more profound than himself. A 'soul' inhabits him and brings him to existence, which is itself a factor in the mastery that power exercises over the body. The soul is the effect and instrument of a political anatomy; the soul is the prison of the body."[12] Subjection, in a moral as well as in a physical sense, is carried out by means of a dual functioning of discourse which, on the one hand, socializes bodies by making them amenable to the effects of a second purpose—which is the definition and organization of the restraints and coercions to be applied. There are, of course, the ever-present areas of self-interest that are co-opted by the process in the name of certain truths. This is accomplished through an appeal to a reason capable of discerning truths by virtue of its disinterested and "objective" nature.

We have already seen how, in the modern configuration of epistemological processes, knowledge achieves its claims of universality and imposes its mastery through the circularity of the analytic of finitude, according to which the empirical and the ontological orders are fundamentally identical and different at the same time: they are identical because an intuitive a priori justifies knowledge; they are different because the legitimation of the empirical, the contingent, is carried out in terms of universal themes. The strategy employed by the human sciences illustrates particularly well the ambiguous position of modern discourse on man, because they "occupy the distance that separates (though not without connecting them) biology, economics, and philology from that which gives them possibility in the very being of man."[13] They partake of the strategy an analytic of finitude imposes on the modern age: they both link and separate being and positive knowledge, they are identity and difference at the same time. The subterfuge is possible because the Other is called on to fulfill two functions: it is the ineffable a priori as well as the ultimate referent. "Man," as the subject and object of modern humanistic discourse is, as Foucault points out, both the source of empirical data as well as the transcendental guarantee for the truth of the data. As a consequence, "because he is an empirico-transcendental doublet, man is also the locus of misunderstanding—of misunderstanding that constantly exposes his thought to the risk of being swamped by his own being, and also enables him to recover his integrity on the basis of what eludes him."[14] Foucault's critique, in this perspective, can be construed as an attempt to valorize precisely what escapes human thought, because it is in this direction that lies the hope of escaping the dogmatism of modern discourse: instead of turning thought inward toward an ever-renewed confirmation of its validity, Foucault wishes to direct it to the otherness of the pure being of language, a language devoid of sense:

From the moment . . . when discourse ceases to follow the incline of a thought that interiorizes itself and, addressing itself to the very being of language, turns thought back to the outside, it is . . . —a language about the outside of all language, words about the invisible side of words; and aware of what already exists in language, what has already been said, printed, manifested, —listening, not so much to what has been pronounced in it but to the void circulating between its words, to the murmur that never stops undoing it, it is a discourse about the non-discourse of all language, a fiction of the invisible space where it appears.[15]

This attraction to the strange otherness which Foucault found in the work of such writers as Blanchot is understandable in light of his conviction that "it is no longer possible to think in our day other than in the void left by man's disappearance."[16] This void is the otherness that Foucault himself sought to empower.

The strikingly paradoxical nature of such an undertaking is one of the aspects in Foucault's philosophy that has made critics see it as fundamentally postmodern in its strategy and outlook. Indeed, Foucault's approach captures a dilemma that is fundamental to postmodern thought: in shaping a new form of thought, he was attempting to extricate himself from the *savoir* that informed his thinking, from everything that had given his thought its particular shape and configuration. That is why Foucault's attitude toward this *savoir* is ambiguous. He sees it as a realm at the limits of consciousness, a dimension apt to fascinate with its power to mold as well as to alienate with its potential for control and oppression. The justification for this ambivalence is to be found in the realization that all knowledge derives from a dimension both profound and elusive with which it is organically linked: "In a society, all knowledge, philosophical ideas, everyday opinions, but also institutions, commercial and police practices, customs, everything is related to a certain *savoir* that is implicit in and characteristic of this society."[17] This *savoir* is thus a condition of possibility, a cognitive matrix that organizes different fields of knowledge and legitimates truths. When truths cease to command a general adherence, the underlying epistemological organization of an epoch becomes vulnerable to critique: the obsolescent condition of the disintegrating "order of things" is all the more open to criticism when it continues to hold a partial sway over the critic. It is in this situation that a critique of culture becomes, at the same time, an attempt to escape identity, to get away from oneself—an injunction to "se déprendre de soi."

Foucault does not deny that the desire to "se déprendre de soi" is an imperative that has its roots in some very personal experiences. It has something to do, for example, with a growing feeling of alienation toward intellectual currents whose stifling domination Foucault experienced in his youth. He explains: "I belong to a generation of people who, when they were students, were shut in within the boundaries of a horizon demarcated by Marxism, phenomenology, existentialism, etc. All very interesting, stimulating things but which, after a while, bring on a feeling of suffocation and the desire to go look somewhere else."[18] In a similar manner, recalling his early professional involvement with psychiatry, Foucault remembers vividly the sensation of being an outsider, of not being able to think according to and within the accepted codes of psychiatric knowledge. He remembers, for example, the suffering he experienced at the sight of the inmates' suffering, a feeling of empathy that contrasted sharply with the scientific impassivity of the doctors.[19] What he calls his "good fortune" of finding himself in a psychiatric hospital "neither as a patient nor as a doctor" gave him also the opportunity to observe the goings-on with "a somewhat empty, a somewhat neutral gaze . . . outside the codes . . . to become conscious of this extremely strange reality of confinement."[20] The distance provided by his disinvolvement gave him a vantage from which he was able to observe the professionals in action. What struck Foucault was the manner in which the act of confining human beings was taken as something perfectly natural, as a procedure whose legitimacy was self-evident. The naturalness of this power to subject others led him to reflect on the long historical process that had yielded the necessary truths for institutionalizing procedures of confinement. In a sense then, the alienation, even revulsion occasioned by certain ways of applying knowledge made Foucault eager to examine more closely the history, mechanisms, and effects of this knowledge.

It is of course relatively recently that Foucault arrived at such a comprehensive understanding of the motives that guided the writing of his earlier works in particular. At the same time, it is significant that it is also in the light of these earlier experiences that he explains the most recent project on sexuality, noting that too much has been made of a supposed contrast between his earlier and his later writings. "I have said nothing different from what I was already saying," he observes, and points out that by studying the manner of "governing" the insane, he was attempting to connect the "constitution of the experience of the self by someone insane, within the framework of mental illness, to psychiatric practice and the institution of the asylum." In his books on sexuality, he wanted to "show how the governing of the self is integrated in a practice of governing others." In both cases, the aim was the same because it was to find out "how an 'experience' made up of the relations to self and others is constituted."[21]

What is noteworthy here is that the problematic of the subject has been extended to include a consideration of "others." The question of the subject had always been a central one in Foucault's work, but it became especially crucial when he discovered that the problematization of the subject becomes an issue only with the advent of Christianity. The constitution of the self as subject had evidently not posed a problem in antiquity because, although there was a *mode d'asujettissement*—a mode of subjection—it was something that did not operate so much according to moral norms as it was determined by an aesthetic choice and a political system. What intrigued Foucault at this juncture was the process of transformation that led from a highly personalized ethic to the Christian kind of morality with its interdictions and normalizing effects.

Foucault was indeed looking for a connection between the two eras in question—antiquity and early Christianity—not so much in terms of a break separating them but from the perspective of a continuity to be found in a transposition of elements. These elements, although different when considered separately, seemed to fit into patterns that performed the same function for both ages. Thus, Foucault points out that, although the notion of discontinuity had always been an important methodological tool for him, its significance has always been exaggerated by critics; he singles out instead the notion of problematization as the thematic thread linking all his analyses to a common purpose. The point, he argues, is not to find divergences and to bring out oppositions but to gain a better understanding of cultural processes by trying to see, as much as possible, the whole panorama—both synchronically and diachronically—because "it is the ensemble of discursive and nondiscursive practices which brings something to the interplay of truths and falsehoods constituting it into an object of thought."[22] It is, then, the comparative approach that is the most likely to furnish a different grasp of the *savoir* that oversees knowledge-power formations and determines a cultural identity.

It is also in this context that the knowledges Foucault resurrects become useful: they are neither exemplary nor privileged but serve to alter acquired and naturalized perspectives. Thus, when Foucault talks of the Greeks it is not to present them as models for a lifestyle. Indeed, considering their elitism, the institution of slavery, and the exclusiveness of male privilege that characterize Greek society, Foucault admits to a feeling of contempt for the Greek ethics of pleasure, which he sees irrevocably "linked to a virile society, to nonsymmetry, exclusion of the other, an obsession with penetration, and a kind of threat of being dispossessed of your own energy, and so on."[23] However, when the Greek episode becomes an integral component of the genealogy of a specific problematic, it has a valuable contribution to make to a current perception of subjectivity. For example, Foucault discovers that "the great changes which occurred between Greek society, Greek ethics, Greek morality and how the Christians viewed themselves are not in the code but are in what I call the 'ethics,' the relation to oneself."[24] This relation to oneself has been the unstated, unacknowledged part of a massive *savoir* whose visible manifestation is the code that stipulates what is forbidden and what is not. To see a pattern in the way transformations have taken place not in the code but in the manner a relation to oneself is conceived can be helpful for understanding the nature of present-day approaches to the problem of ethics. Foucault thinks that in this sense our problem could be similar to that of the Greeks "since most of us no longer believe that ethics is founded in religion"; our concerns are more like those of the ancient Greeks because "in Greek ethics people were concerned with their moral conduct, their ethics, their relations to themselves and to others much more than with religious problems."[25] Thus Foucault brings out once more the impossibility of considering separately a relation to oneself and relations with others and concludes that the Christian model, understood as "a moral experience centered on the subject no longer seems satisfactory."[26]

In the case of Foucault's own relation to himself, of his self-perception as intellectual in particular, the problematization is similar. The effort to "make oneself permanently able to unbind oneself from oneself [se rendre capable en permanence de se déprendre de soi-même]"—has, as its corollary, a concomitant effort to involve others. Consequently, "this effort to modify your own thinking and that of others . . . seems to be the intellectual's raison d'être."[27] The intellectual's purpose is not to propose models or to "shape the political will of others; it is . . . to reexamine evidences and postulates, to shake up habits, ways of doing and thinking, to dissipate accepted familiarities, to reexamine rules and institutions, and by taking as a starting point this reproblematization (in which he plays his specific role of intellectual) to take part in the formation of a political will (where he has his role of citizen to play)."[28]

This reaffirmation of the already familiar choice of specific over the universal intellectual stance brings up the theme of identity once more—but with an additional specification: that of citizenship. According to Foucault, the intellectual is someone involved with concrete issues and subject to the same constraints as other citizens. The awareness of these constraints joined to the desire to elucidate them gives the intellectual's task its specificity. This task, which is at once an effort to lift subjection by displaying its mechanisms and to unbind oneself from oneself by undertaking to constantly transform one's own thinking, is also an attempt to locate the intellectual's freedom at the point of his or her limitations—the point at which desire meets with processes of subjectivization, the place where identity forms. To elucidate these processes, the appropriate questions to ask are, "Who makes decisions for me? Who keeps me from doing one thing and tells me to do something else? Who programs my movements and my schedule? Who forces me to live at this particular place while I work at this other one? How are these decisions that completely articulate my life made?"[29] There are two observations to be made with regard to Foucault's choice of questions. First, they are not asked in order to uncover a specific identity, a person, group, or class lurking behind each "who"; only a "universal" intellectual would attempt or claim to do this. For Foucault, there are no strategists to be identified behind the strategies—no one occupies the place of the Other. Nevertheless, it is in the name of the Other that identities are formed; by questioning the source of the forces that control an individual's life,

Foucault calls into question the accepted patterns of individualization.

Secondly, the questions suggested by Foucault are the kind that anyone could ask and yet they are highly improbable questions: they go counter to some of the most deeply ingrained and culturally conditioned assumptions concerning individual freedom and responsibility. Thus it is the intellectual's obligation to make others aware of questions and possibilities that some would call unacceptable or inconceivable. The problematization of the intellectual's role is inextricably linked to the problematization of the place humans occupy in society, a place designated and defined by a cultural and social order; the "souci de soi" is but an integral part of a "souci des autres." Foucault once characterized his intellectual stance as one of "hyper- and pessimistic activism."[30] It is a description that alludes to the unresolvable tension between sameness and alterity, between identity and the desire to be different, that characterizes the place of the intellectual's questioning in Foucault's work. There are no solutions or victories to be anticipated, only a constant resistance to be maintained—one we find expressed once more on the back cover of Foucault's last two books, in a quotation from the poet René Char: "L'histoire des hommes est la longue succession des synonymes d'un même vocable. Y contredire est un devoir."

Fundamental to this logic is the recognition of the fact that reality is ineffable and that "the symbolic order creates its own realities according to its own laws." Foucault, for example, "took seriously Lacan's insistence that all that we know, all that we do, and all that we are is predetermined by the possibilities inherent in the symbolic order."[31] What he wanted to develop was an approach focusing on the mechanisms that become operative in the symbolic order to produce subjects. Foucault explained:

> What interested me . . . were precisely the forms of rationality applied by the human subject to itself . . . the question I asked myself was this: how is it that the human subject took itself as the object of possible knowledge? Through what forms of rationality and historical conditions? And finally at what price? This is my question: at what price can subjects speak the truth about themselves? . . . An ensemble of complex, staggered elements where you find that institutional game-playing, class relations, professional conflicts, mo-

dalities of knowledge and, lastly, a whole history of the subject of reason are involved.[32]

Foucault thus tried to bring to light what had remained hidden under the cover of an all-powerful consciousness by problematizing the self-evident and by effecting reversals in all our familiar ways of thinking and doing. In addition, Foucault teaches us a lesson in modesty by showing us that our philosophy is much less competent, and that things are much more complicated, than we had suspected. At the same time, he refuses to indulge in nostalgia or anxiety: "In Foucault, the finiteness of man's thought is not a tragic fate, but a comic celebration of the ridiculousness of human pretensions to universal knowledge and universal truth."[33] Paradoxically, the importance of intellectual work is not diminished by this realization. Foucault also understands that truth has become an "increasingly important commodity" in our civilization; it is fabricated, manipulated, disseminated, and inculcated as never before. He once remarked that the point of his investigations was not to show "that everything is bad, but that everything is dangerous."[34] Consequently, intellectuals needed to be aware of a possible collusion between their work and dominant and oppressive discourses and institutions. Of course, Foucault was not the only structuralist to appreciate this point; thinkers like Barthes and Derrida also taught us to see that "the subject continues to repeat the institutional languages, the cultural fragments, the *epistemes,* the norms, the rules, the writings, the re-presentations and the myths of a symbolic order which remains essentially independent of human beings and which creates reality as we know it."[35] They also challenged the proposition that we can dominate and shape this reality through force of intellect.

The desire to dominate reality is an imperative at the heart of modern thought and is itself a mode of action; it is a pure will to knowledge that precludes the kind of contemplative strategy necessary for elaborating a genuine ethics. Foucault finds that "the historical analysis of this rancorous will to knowledge reveals that all knowledge rests upon injustice . . . and that the instinct for knowledge is malicious. . . . Even in the greatly expanded form it assumes today, the will to knowledge does not achieve a universal truth; man is not given an exact and serene mastery of nature. . . . its development is not tied to the constitution and affirmation of a free subject; rather, it creates a progressive enslavement to its instinctive violence."[36] Accordingly, the critic's major responsibility is to "problematize" the processes through which truth is produced and its applications are rationalized because "in its constitutive process, 'reason' in and of itself is violence: the regime of truth in some ways represents its concealment."[37] Thus Foucault sees his own work as an attempt to elaborate a genealogy of *problématiques,* as a project intended to bring out the problematic aspects of the procedures that oversee the production, dissemination, and application of truths. The purpose is to reveal all the unstated presuppositions, the unquestioned and dubious rationales, and the self-serving interests that attend the production of truth.

At the same time, Foucault reminds us, the critic has to be aware that the procedures in question often depend on circumstances and forces outside the realm of anyone's perception and understanding—even the critic's. The intellectual can never pretend to be "above it all" and has an obligation ceaselessly to problematize his or her own position. Consequently, Foucault's critical enterprise is thoroughly informed by his perception of his own role and function as intellectual. His approach to the systems of thought he seeks to survey takes into account both the limits imposed on him and the obligation to expose the limitations of knowledge and morality. In short, Foucault's ethic is a function of his critical project: it makes him conceive of his role as critic in terms of a responsibility toward himself as well as toward others.

CHAPTER 4

INTERPRETING FOUCAULT

W HEN MICHEL FOUCAULT was once asked whether he considered himself a postmodern thinker, he responded by saying that he did not know what the term *postmodern* meant: Foucault was simply indicating that he was not interested in the issue of postmodernism. It is therefore ironic that he should have become, after his death, an exemplary postmodernist. On the other hand, this is hardly surprising: Foucault clearly helped set the terms and outline the issues of an emerging movement in the history of Western thought, a mode of thinking that tends to be identified, retrospectively, as postmodernism. This contribution and influence can best be appreciated in the context of the continuing debate on the significance and validity of Foucault's work. It is a dispute that can also help clear up some of the confusion arising from conflicting interpretations of postmodern critical practices. Viewed in the context of the debate on the legitimacy of Foucault's theories, the postmodernism associated with poststructuralist critique acquires the specification of a post–Enlightenment, post–Marxist, and postliberal political and philosophical mode of thought.

Simply put, the central issue between Foucault's supporters and his critics is the question of the relationship of society and the world to our knowledge. While the critics base their objections on a model of a conscious and purposeful subject whose agency has a direct and verifiable impact on the order of things, defenders of Foucault are increasingly interested in elaborating an insight that was central to Foucault's work: the realization that before we attempt to influence events or change the world, it behooves us to take into account, to examine, and to elucidate what mediates between us and our representation of reality. To do this, we must first be cured of our illusions about our ability to determine or ratify truth; yet we must also recognize our undeniable aptitude to produce "truth-effects." Foucault explains: "I am fully aware that I have never written anything other than fictions. For all that, I would not want to say that they are outside truth. It seems possible to me to make fiction work within truth, to induce truth-effects within a fictional discourse, and in some way to make the discourse of truth arouse, 'fabricate' something which does not as yet exist, thus 'fiction' something. One 'fictions' history starting from a political reality that renders it true, one 'fictions' a politics that doesn't as yet exist starting from an historical truth."[1]

In addition, one needs constantly to confront one's fictional creations with the historical and discursive regime of truths within and against which they are elaborated. That is why Foucault emphasized that he had "always been concerned with linking together as tightly as possible the historical and theoretical analysis of power relations, institutions, and knowledge, to the movements, critiques, and experiences that call them into question in reality."[2] Foucault was generally opposed to systematic, totalizing approaches to human affairs and considered it essential to confront thought with the concrete evidence of our experience of the "order of things." It is this approach that has given his work the designation "postmodern" and has placed it in close affinity with the increasingly numerous and important other attempts at disclosing strategies of truth-effects in our culture and society. It is also this postmodern propensity for privileging the discontinuous and the dissonant that has motivated a considerable resistance to Foucault's thought.

Some of the more familiar objections raised to Foucault's writings amount to a refusal to grant what is a fundamental insight proposed by the philosopher: the very bases for criticism have changed and it is no longer possible, or useful, to proceed according to standards of rationality inherited from earlier ages. The anthology of critical appraisals, *Foucault: A Critical Reader,* edited by David Couzens Hoy and published six years ago, still provides the most instructive illustration of the confrontation Foucault's writings have occasioned around the ideologies inspired by the

Enlightenment. At first, Hoy tells us, his purpose had been to assemble "careful counterarguments to Foucault's own theses" and to invite Foucault's response to them. This plan was revised following the unexpected death of the philosopher and the book "now includes essays that are useful in rebutting some common criticisms by showing that his ideas are not what the standard objections assume them to be."[3] As a result, the misunderstandings and misrepresentations that have become standard in critical approaches to Foucault's work are themselves highlighted and rebutted in the same volume by those critics who find his insights valuable.

The principal result of this confrontation is to demonstrate that the axiological foundation on which detractors elaborate their critiques constitutes the force as well as the principal deficiency of their arguments. The most common and seemingly most effective reproach aimed at Foucault's enterprise is the claim that his critical position is self-contradictory, therefore, incoherent. It is alleged that, in spite of everything he says, Foucault cannot help subscribing to the very values he critiques since he has no other value system to offer in their place. That is, so the argument goes, Foucault has to stand *somewhere:* he is either with us or against us— and if he is against the system, he has to identify a position outside it as the preferred alternative. Second, Foucault's notion of power, it is claimed, makes no sense—especially in light of the stipulation that relations of power can be both intentional and nonsubjective. History, according to Charles Taylor, is made up of purposeful human action; therefore, any "undesigned systematicity has to be related to the purposeful action of agents in a way that we can understand"; this is because, as a rule, "all patterns have to be made *intelligible* in relation to conscious action." Systematicity is unimaginable without "the purposeful human action in which it arose and which it has come to shape."[4]

Critics such as Michael Walzer, Charles Taylor, Jürgen Habermas, and others would like to see Foucault recognize the positive aspects of the Western tradition and espouse their own faith in a rationality informed by common sense and democratic ideals. Thus we are told that Foucault's model "*does not make sense* without at least the idea of liberation," that it offers no real hope of resisting or overturning domination.[5] Moreover, Foucault's account of the workings of power is simply too one-sided, too negative—thus incoherent because it fails to recognize everything progressive, positive, and admirable in the historical evolution of our civilization; it "leaves out everything in Western history which has been animated by civic humanism or analogous movements."[6] This alleged shortcoming of Foucault's analyses is deemed particularly glaring in the context of other systems, other societies, that do not enjoy our freedoms and advantages; thus, Foucault's "account of the carceral archipelago contains no hint of how or why our own society stops short of the Gulag. For such an account would require what Foucault always resists: some positive evaluation of the liberal state."[7] In a similar vein, Sheldon Wolin has chastised Foucault for not recognizing how much better off we are today than our ancestors with our "roads, bridges, schools" and "phenomenal growth of scientific knowledge and its practical applications."[8]

These requirements of coherence and grateful appreciation amount to a demand that Foucault renounce precisely the part of his project that has been recognized as having the most innovative and far-reaching critical potential. In a. sense, Foucault's critics would have liked to see Foucault undo what he had accomplished, for "these ways of reading Foucault have in common a reassertion of metaphysical patterns and ideas that are destabilized in Foucault's thought."[9] Of course, from Foucault's perspective, any recourse to established values, to notions of progress and civilized achievement, implies a reliance on a precritical framework that provides the answer to problems before the question is even posed. Furthermore, a systematicity made intelligible is suspect by definition: it is a post facto justification that is valid only because it fits the requirements of the existing regime of truth; as Foucault puts it, "truth consists of a certain relationship that discourse or knowledge has with itself."[10] Similarly, all explanations proposing clearly defined cause–effect links are suspect because they discount anything outside the boundaries of what currently passes the test of intelligibility. As a consequence, the notion of "intelligibility" as well as the criteria used for making human activity intelligible constitutes the very problem to be addressed. David R. Hiley argues that Foucault's critics end up reproducing the pattern of nineteenth-century humanism which, as Foucault showed, was endlessly caught in the tautology of "man and his doubles: from man as the condition for the possibility of knowledge to man as himself an object in the empirical field." Any promise of emancipation is an illusion in the context of this pattern: "In terms of Foucault's anti-humanism, Habermas and Taylor are not only caught up in the futility of the doubles—Habermas' empirical theory of communication competency as the flip side of a transcendental grounding of rationality and Taylor's grounding of political rationality in the self-interpreting character of human beings and in intersubjective meanings as a privilege of man—but they are part of the very danger of normalization."[11]

When critics reproach Foucault for not respecting rationality and the values accompanying it, they implicitly discount the value and relevancy of questions that had become unavoidable for him: "*What* is this Reason that we use? What are its historical effects? What are its limits, and what are its dangers? How can we exist as rational beings, fortunately committed to practicing a rationality that is unfortunately crisscrossed by intrinsic dangers?"[12] For Foucault's critics, these dangers are nonexistent since they will not allow—what is fundamental to Foucault's way of seeing—that the events marking human existence are determined at a level not amenable to well-intentioned and rational methods of oversight and control. Thus Walzer discounts the originality of Foucault's critique of normalization by arguing that "the triumph of professional or scientific norms over legal rights and of local discipline over constitutional law is a fairly common theme of contemporary social criticism."[13] That is, from Walzer's perspective, Foucault's critique makes sense only on a level of a commonsensical, reformist discourse—the kind, precisely, that Walzer believes in. Therefore, when Foucault points out that his goal in defending the rights of prisoners "was not to extend the visiting rights of prisoners to 30 minutes or to procure flush toilets for the cells, but to question the social and moral distinction between the innocent and the guilty," Walzer can only conclude that Foucault is "a moral as well as a political anarchist. For him morality and politics go together."[14] The scandalized tone of Walzer's reproach is amusing if we consider that what he deems unthinkable is at the very core of Foucault's project: Foucault stated explicitly that what interested him really was morals rather than politics "or, in any case, politics as an ethics."[15] Walzer is of course not alone in deploring Foucault's "anarchism." In a similar vein, others have pointed to Foucault's unrelenting "pessimism" and deplored his "nihilism."

As a number of essayists in Hoy's volume make clear, the failure to think things through is to be found less in Foucault than in the analyses of his critics. The more recent work of Charles E. Scott and James W. Bernauer further demonstrates that Foucault is perfectly coherent in his theorizing. In the first place, Foucault's critics tend to predicate their arguments on an unquestioning and nostalgic reverence for a particular model of human agency; their accusations reveal the hidden source of this attitude: "Optimism, pessimism, nihilism, and the like are all concepts that make sense only within the idea of a transcendental or enduring subject."[16] Also, as Bernauer points out, because "we are heirs to an ideophilia, a love of an ideal intelligibility," anything threatening this comfortable ideal will be discounted and resisted.[17] Since they operate on the basis of a system of values they consider unimpeachable, Foucault's critics generally fail to question the agenda informing their own critique; thus, for example, Habermas's attacks on Foucault have typically ignored the postwar German sociopolitical agenda motivating them. John Rajchman has argued that Habermas's "Germanic misconstrual" of Foucault is clearly attributable to the German philosopher's failure to pay "attention to the 'context' in which he himself is reading the work of the neostructuralists."[18] The arguments of the critics are tactical in the sense that they are devised to protect a whole system in danger of collapsing. But they are also made vulnerable by the very logic sustaining them.

Thus, in trying to rescue modernity from its subverters, Habermas posits a "communicative rationality" that oversees and arbitrates the transmission of moral values. As we saw earlier, he launched an attack on the neo-Nietzschean strain in the French critical tradition by stigmatizing its representatives with the label "neoconservatives." A number of critics have found this accusation ironic because "it is Habermas's critique of postmodernism and its foundationalist drive that shows a spontaneous alliance with a traditionalist, conservative fundamentalism of basic values and basic norms."[19] The attempt to set up an ultimate frame of reference that will serve as a guarantee for our rationality forgets the valuable lesson of Nietzsche, who taught us that a " 'logic' of reason both betrays and masks the logic of the living man." Nietzsche also showed that the project of subsuming the "changing, intolerable, unassimilable world as such" under the transcendental category of "Reason" amounts to adopting the characteristically conservative tactic of imposing "the necessity of a 'Being,' of a 'substance' uncontaminated by becoming and evolution" in an attempt to transform "this world into an intelligible world, a world of stable identities, available to knowledge."[20] Such an enterprise appears as a distinctly regressive tactic in comparison with the work done by Derrida, for example, for whom "the subject of political philosophy is the question of reason, that is to say, the question about the ability of an account of rationality to be open to the need to question the notion of reason."[21]

Foucault also rejected the notion of an objective, uncontaminated, normative standpoint existing outside the realm of one's investigations because the constitution of a knowledge was, for him, a process involving the simultaneous constitution of a knowing subject; he viewed this concern as central to his work, explaining, in 1978: "Everything that I have occupied myself with up till now essentially regards the way in which people in Western societies have had experiences that were used in the process of knowing a determinate, objective set of things while at the same time constituting themselves as subjects under fixed and determinate conditions."[22] A claim of an objective standpoint could be nothing less than magical: it would imply that the critic who is tied to a concrete historical and social development, who speaks the language of a particular culture and morality, can somehow and suddenly be set free from all contingency and dependency and, rising above the cultural and political circumstances enabling his very critique, find himself serenely dispensing his judgment in the name of eternal and universal truths. Scott finds this approach fundamentally disabled by "a torsion of laws that have their authority by virtue of a given lineage and that order all random things within their jurisdiction as though they derived their force from outside their heritage."[23] To ignore the interpretative move that sustains one's critical approach is to impose one's arguments authoritatively; thus Dreyfus and Rabinow propose that "Habermas's refusal to admit his indebtedness to interpretation makes his position professoral."[24]

Another reason for rejecting Foucault's work has been based on practical considerations of political effectiveness. Critics argue that it is impossible to accept Foucault's analyses because they offer no hope of resisting, of changing or reforming any system that might be deemed oppressive. Walzer points out that Foucault neither adopts the codes and categories of his social system nor proposes new ones; as a consequence, "that refusal, which makes his genealogies so powerful and so relentless, is also the catastrophic weakness of his political theory."[25] Such a critique once more refuses to entertain the possibility that the world and society might function differently from the version to which it subscribes implicitly. Of course, when relations between patterns of conscious action and the concatenation of events can be made intelligible, clear distinctions can be established between the rational and the irrational, right and wrong, guilt and innocence. Foucault showed that such distinctions are determined in ways that are not always evident, rational, or self-consciously purposeful and consistent. It is precisely when rational intelligibility imposes itself as all-encompassing and self-sufficient that power strategies operating outside the limits of immediate comprehension are given free rein. It is for this reason that Foucault's defense of the rights of prisoners meant to question "the social and moral distinction between the innocent and the guilty"—a distinction determined far less objectively, less rationally than well-meaning defenders of the Western democratic system like to imagine. Foucault's refusal to play according to the guidelines his critics consider valid can be considered deficient only if the world does indeed operate according to the universal values and abstract model implicit in the reformist, liberal political strategy espoused by Walzer and others.

Procedures of abstraction and universalization occlude the contingent nature of events, disguising it with slogans; this pattern was established at the end of the eighteenth century, when the French Revolution and its aftermath ended up defining social existence in terms of "a theoretical liberty and an abstract equality, while at the same time it created a social system that effectively suppresses this equality and liberty."[26] Talk of freedom is meaningless unless thought is freed from its philosophically, politically, and ethically imposed confinement and thus is given the opportunity to realize the historical contingency of the real. Foucault's great accomplishment, according to Bernauer, has been to "free thought from a search for formal structures and place it in an historical field where it must confront the singular, contingent, and arbitrary that operate in what is put forward as universal, necessary, and obligatory." In this way, the function of the "*savoir* dimension" of thought is made apparent: it is a dimension that is inevitably "bound up with social and political practices," since it shapes knowledge and decisions even before they are made by determining situations to be analyzed and the remedies to be prescribed.[27]

For a growing number of scholars, then, it is the refusal to play according to the established rules that is the most promising and valuable aspect of a Foucaultian approach. This refusal requires a fundamental rethinking of our relation to our thought and to our subjectivity; and it relocates transcendence from the realm of subjective certitude to the agency of the symbolic: "For Foucault, there is a transcendence that is not that of a subject, or of a universal framework of discourse, but rather that of the events in the particular discourses of which we are capable at a time and place. Such transcendence is thus not ideal and timeless but material and ever-changing. It is the 'it poses itself' of a question in the midst of the assumptions upon which our knowledge, our procedures, our agreements rest."[28] The recognition of this "material and ever-changing" transcendence at the level of discourse and discursive events also requires that we recognize "the effect of nonsystematizable randomness that moves through a systematic discourse" and that we modify our faith in our capacity to influence or to change the world around us.[29] To ignore this randomness and arbitrariness is to help legitimize those processes of selection, segregation, and hierarchization that are essential in strategies of self-maintenance and self-determination. Modern forms of knowledge are predicated on an amnesia that allows them to operate by forgetting their beginnings, the exclusions and other violent devices used to establish legitimacy. That is why Foucault's analyses work as a "counter-memory" by showing that Western reason has appropriated what it cannot really control. Reason has assimilated the seeds of its own destruction by ignoring its own unreasonable attempt to impose a scheme on everything that lay outside its domain: "Values carry with them their own formative processes. . . . The ascetic ideal, for example, embodies both life-affirmation and life-denial. The ethical subject embodies both autonomy and subjection. Authenticity embodies both self-realization and self-deconstruction."[30] The eventual contradictions and conflicts that emerge in a given system of values are produced by what Scott characterizes as a "self-overcoming recoil." Scott credits Foucault with exploiting this propensity for self-questioning inherent in our very tradition and finds that "self-overcoming and recoil characterize his thought and give his genealogies an import that goes considerably beyond the specific claims that he makes."[31]

In elaborating itself on the basis of what formed it and in separating itself from that formation, Foucault's discourse cannot claim to impose a program or to recommend a correct line of action. The value of his work is attributable to its manner of questioning itself, of questioning the very tradition that has given rise to it. As Arnold Davidson rightly points out, for Foucault, the rules determining our discursive practices are "never formulated by the participants in the discursive practices; they are not available to their consciousness, but constitute . . . the 'positive unconscious' of knowledge."[32] There are, then, two kinds of operations of knowledge—one conscious, rational, visible but superficial, serving to promote official goals and programs; the other unconscious—unobtrusive but most influential, determining moral norms and legitimating epistemological principles and standards. Ian Hacking explains that "Foucault used the French word *connaissance* to stand for such items of surface knowledge, while *savoir* meant more than science; it was a frame, postulated by Foucault, within which surface hypotheses got their sense."[33] For Foucault, the official representation of values was deceiving because he understood that "broad, impersonal social and historical developments may have little direct connection with what agents chose to do or what they think they are doing." In consequence, "as a historian he wants to point to a level below the explicit moral precepts or other factors that are for the most part reflectively available to individual agents."[34]

Thought does not translate directly into action, therefore, nor do actions enjoy a transitive relation to the configuration of discursive and nondiscursive practices. There is always an insuperable gap between our intentions and events because thought "cannot replace or adequately imitate nonthinking life, that is, most of life."[35] The modern mode of representation has provided the unity and continuity necessary for maintaining the illusion of effective agency. Foucault demonstrated how the concept of "man" was instrumental in the nineteenth century in covering up the discontinuity between consciousness and the experience of everyday life; this cover-up was part of an attempt to produce a definitive and synthetic mode of knowledge: the result has been the dissolution of the "analytic of finitude" and the realization that "Man, in spite of its goal to provide unity, means discontinuity between itself and what it knows."[36] "Man" thus becomes a void; it is the gap or discontinuity that has suddenly been revealed between being and knowing. Consequently, in the postmodern context, the individual can no longer claim the essence of a "being": the newly emerging consciousness, "trapped by its representational activity, knows itself only as a representation, never as the pre-representational unity that it has to be."[37] The event bringing about this new awareness is then the force of the ever-changing configuration of discourse. And a discourse of reason was bound to produce the very questioning that eventually invalidated its claim to intellectual hegemony.

Foucault has argued that modernity was incapable of producing a morality that was other than self-referential. In this, it followed the pattern set by reason, which was ignorant of its own unreasonable attempt to impose a rational scheme on the world under the pretense that it would keep the irrational at bay. Foucault also believed that, in an effort to hide the arbitrariness of their claims, strategies of self-maintenance and self-determination became inevitably authoritative, even violent; his analyses can therefore be seen to be motivated by what Scott calls a general "guiding suspicion" underlying the critique of modernity, the suspicion that "the self-determination of our culture makes inevitable the suffering and destruction to which it is insensitive not only by virtue of its specific values, but also by virtue of the manner of self-determination that we broadly call ethics. The issue is obscure because we are thoroughly a part of the process and structures of value that fall into question."[38]

Traditional morality was established as a mode of self-constitution and self-mastery and was, at the same time, a "denial of the liberty of its lineage" because "self-mastery means in practice internalized domination of an individual by given rules and principles that support the interests of specific groups of people." The apparent self-contradiction of an ideal of self-mastery that works as a device of control is resolved in the light of Foucault's concept of power-knowledge strategies: these are inherent in the games of truth and error that determine what people think since "what people know to be true and how they influence and control each other—the power they exercise with regard to each other—are inseparably linked."[39] Real freedom, on the other hand, is to be found in "the continuous reversibility and substitutability of things. The liberty of the subject, for example, is not found primarily as freedom of choice or as an anxious relation of subjectivity to an infinite other. It is found in part as the historical and optional development of self-constitution." Finally, because the truth of the subject is determined in the context of games of truth and error, "the priority of the subject is also reversed, and the subject is found to derive from games of truth and power."[40]

Foucault's notable contribution has been to illuminate a particular aspect of our society and to modify a traditional view that has been increasingly incapable of accounting for the effects of power-knowledge strategies in our societies: "The modern state does not constitute a monolith confronting individuals from above, but a 'matrix of individualization' which forms, shapes and governs individuality through the exercise of a new form of 'pastoral power' over the social." The modern state is characterized by "the development of individualizing techniques and practices which are reducible neither to force nor to consent, techniques and practices which have transformed political conflict and struggle through the constitution of new forms of social cohesion."[41] What makes Foucault's critical theory effective is his manner of conceptualizing power: he does not understand power as a tangible thing, as something one possesses and applies, but suggests that "power is to be taken nominalistically—not as a real substance or as a property, but simply as a name for a complex strategy or grid of intelligibility."[42] In this light, it makes perfect sense to characterize power as something that is both intentional and nonsubjective, because the grid of power does not originate in any one individual and the subject situates itself strategically within the grid.

The problem with modernity and its representation of relations of power, as Bernauer sees it, is that "the modern subject was fashioned in isolation from ethical and aesthetic concerns."[43] The truth determining one's place in society could therefore serve to

hide the politics of truth that presided over society's constitution—
the economic, ideological, scientific, and institutional strategies
that determine the worth of individuals, the professional, racial,
sexual, and class hierarchies that legitimize the possession of privilege and justify the lack thereof. In light of this understanding,
Foucault saw clearly that "present political struggles must 'revolve
around the question: Who are we? They are a refusal of these
abstractions, of economic and ideological state violence . . . also a
refusal of a scientific or administrative inquisition which determines who one is.' "[44] Furthermore, it is precisely because the
subject is, after all, a void, an empty representation, that we are not
hopelessly trapped within the confines of a system too powerful or
too clever to resist. What traps us is the belief in an essential,
subjective reality; the potential for liberation therefore lies in the
realization that the identity of the subject is no more than an alibi
serving the interests of the dominating order.

Bernauer makes a distinction that brings to our attention one of
the principal sources of the misreadings to which a resistance to
Foucault has given rise: "Foucault's investigations were directed
not to philosophical truth but to the historically true," he points
out.[45] In this regard, Foucault's thought stands opposed to such
modernist paradigms as existentialism and Marxism, philosophies
that "presented themselves as humanisms in which God was replaced by man, and in which an authentic human existence became
an historical possibility." As a result, both "glorified the individual's
historical responsibility."[46] However, considering that the eschatological interpretation of human destiny had simply been replaced
by a teleological one, the urge to uncover the philosophically true
can also be seen as a vestige of a religious ethos, of the priestly
impulse to convert, to judge, and to impose the path to salvation.
Although God was replaced by man, the principal modes of modernist thought retained the earlier theological pattern, patriarchal in
practice and monotheistic in inspiration. As a consequence, the
glorification of the individual's self-determination and responsibility found itself reflected in the modernist propensity to grant
intellectuals a heroic stature. Modernists had a vested interest in the
theme of a subjective plenitude since the belief in effective agency
authorized their own intellectual status, their claim to judge, de-
nounce, and propose change.

For Foucault, this was an oppressive and confining mode of thought. Consequently, his purpose was to discount philosophically attained truths and to dispel the illusion of the heroic status of "man." In doing this, he revealed an unusual and "acute ability to discover and describe the confinements that imprison human life and thought."[47] By revealing the history of the subject, the story of the ways in which subjectivity had been constituted through the ages, Foucault pointed out the politics of truth presiding over the formation of subjects—all the economic, ideological, scientific, and institutional strategies working to determine the identity and worth of individuals, the privileges of the haves and the moral responsibility of the have-nots. Indeed, he was elaborating a new ethics for thought.

CHAPTER 5

THE POSTMODERN CRITIQUE
OF THE ENLIGHTENMENT

We HAVE HAD several occasions already to note that the critical stance postmodernism maintains towards the Enlightenment is motivated by a skeptical view of the legacy of the Age of Reason. Postmodernism manifests a basic distrust of the explanatory schemes and rationales that constitute this legacy and proposes that we reconsider the relative importance of rationality and contingency in the constitution of our social systems and in the elaboration of historical change. Such an approach has become unavoidable, because the powers of conviction yielded by traditional beliefs are seemingly exhausted; thus, "consent to capitalist society (and, perhaps, to any society) it now appears is not a matter of belief at all—or not, at least, belief in foundational, traditional truths."[1] The hope of bringing about radical change by way of rationally orchestrated social upheavals has also diminished because we are beginning to see that "revolutions, in the final account, are not so much things that are made as things that are interrupted and allowed to occur."[2] Considerations of this sort strongly suggest that interpretations and explanations worked out according to a paradigm of thought we have inherited from the eighteenth century are no longer viable and can become counterproductive.

From the perspective of a postmodern critique, reason, which has been modernity's engine, has proven to be fundamentally deficient; specifically, it now appears self-centered and groundless because its legitimacy has been shown to rely solely on its own claim of invulnerability. Reason, we now realize, could never be the universal and objective interpreter of reality that a traditional representation of the Enlightenment once proposed. What was forgotten in the wake of the enthusiasm generated by the Enlightenment was that reason always needs the support of the relations of power and institutions it has created. Thus, the ideals promoted by the Enlightenment were from the start liable to be co-opted by socioeconomic interests and reason could become the special prerogative of a class, race, gender, or nation—that is, of a clearly circumscribed area of political or economic interests that sought to promote its own aims as those of an eternal and essential humanity.

Because we have apparently reached a juncture at which this pretense no longer works, part of the current postmodern vogue can certainly be attributed to the realization that "the idea of thinking the course of history in terms of an *Aufklärung,* of a victory won by reason over the shadows of mythical knowledge, has . . . lost its legitimacy. Demythification is therefore itself considered a myth."[3] The ultimate goal of enlightened reason, which was to make society in some way transparent to itself, is thus revealed to have been the ultimate illusion. What has taken us to this impasse is the failure to account for power—the crucial element complementing and competing with reason. Reason was incapable of guaranteeing the integrity of the Enlightenment project because it had no hold over the workings of power. Worse, it only served to facilitate the operations of power by helping to keep in place the convenient and comforting cover of humanism.

The illusion that had fostered the self-confidence of modern thought having dissipated, what stands out is the contradiction that characterizes our societies; specifically, postmodern critique has made us aware that "Western civilization has been the site of a massive contradiction between its values and its politics, its philosophy and its action, its creed of equality before the law and its actuality of inequality before the fact."[4] With regard to the legacy of the Enlightenment, such an awareness inevitably produces "a realization that the goals and values which have been central to Western 'European' civilization can no longer be considered universal, and that the associated 'project of modernity' is unfinished because its completion is inconceivable and its value in question."[5]

At the same time, this questioning of modernity's value is fraught with a fundamental difficulty: the more postmodern critique questions, the more it becomes aware of its own indebtedness to the object of its critique. One of the principal characteristics of a postmodern critical approach is therefore the ambiguity it displays vis-à-vis modernity. Its strategy can only be that of a "complicitous critique,"[6] to use Linda Hutcheon's term, because it cannot impugn modernity without disavowing its own nature and origins—a pedigree that makes it an integral part of modernity's very history and evolution. The postmodern critical impulse therefore ends up recognizing itself as a strain within modernity, as a critical counterpoint to modernity's self-confident assertiveness, a restraining and willfully debilitating counterinfluence to modernity's aggressive, colonizing activism.

In this regard, it is Michel Foucault who has captured most cogently the dilemma of a postmodern critique of the Enlightenment. More than anyone else perhaps, Foucault was able to appreciate the paradoxical necessity of elaborating a critique of the very thought that has given our capacity for critique its axiological configuration. This awareness of our critical dependency also imposed the need to question the grounds for our questioning: "What is this reason that we use? What are its historical effects? What are its limits, and what are its dangers? How can we exist as rational beings, fortunately committed to practicing a rationality that is unfortunately crisscrossed by intrinsic dangers?"[7]

Moreover, Foucault also suggested that any consideration of the phenomenon of the Enlightenment required not only that we recognize our indebtedness to the ethos of the Age of Enlightenment but that we acknowledge its continuing relevance to our present needs. It is significant, for example, that the course he offered at the Collège de France in 1983—one year before his death—was devoted to a discussion of Kant's essay *Was ist Aufklärung?* Kant's text is important for Foucault, not because it provides an answer to the question it poses, but because it helps delineate the problematic: "Foucault takes the Kantian position merely as a point of departure, as a challenge to develop a new critical ontology of ourselves."[8] Therefore, it was not so much what Kant had to say about the Enlightenment as his manner of posing the problem that intrigues Foucault: "What Foucault finds distinctive and insightful in Kant's essay is a philosopher qua philosopher realizing for the first time that his thinking arises out of and is an attempt to respond to his historical situation."[9]

Foucault recognizes above all the undeniable impact the paradig-matic thought of the Enlightenment has had and continues to have on Western understanding: "It does seem to me that the *Aufklärung,* seen both as a singular event inaugurating modernity and as a permanent process manifesting itself in the history of reason, in the development and instauration of forms of rationality and tech-nique, in the autonomy and authority of knowledge, is not for us simply an episode in the history of ideas. It is a philosophical question inscribed since the eighteenth century in our thought." It is an aspect of our modernity that needs to be problematized by clearly distinguishing the historical singularity of the event from the universal appeal of its ideological content. Foucault believes therefore that "it is not a matter of preserving the remains of the *Aufklärung;* it is the very question of this event as well as its meaning, (the question of the historicity of the thought of univer-sals) that must be kept in mind as that which must be thought."[10]

According to Foucault, in order to get at the present "meaning" of the Enlightenment, it is necessary, first, to separate it from the themes of humanism with which it has been associated since the nineteenth century. Consequently, "the critical question of today has to be turned back into a positive one: in what is given to us as universal, necessary, obligatory, what place is occupied by what-ever is singular, contingent, and the product of arbitrary con-straints?" Such an approach prevents the debate from getting trapped by what Foucault calls the "blackmail of the Enlighten-ment," the idea that "one has to be 'for' or 'against' the Enlighten-ment."[11] An argument about the merits of a system of values—the question of being "for" or "against"—is specious because it elides the questions of the system's ontological status by assuming it is real, that it effectively exists and operates in accordance with its own manner of representing itself.

To develop the needed critical ontology of ourselves, Fou-cault proceeds by questioning traditional explanatory schemes. We should note that in doing this he follows a method the philosophes themselves used as they elaborated their critique of established dogma. Their purpose was to problematize the power relations that derived from claims of revealed truth and to attack the dogmatism evident in the authority to proclaim the truth. They were thus demonstrating that the injunction to " 'obey the will of god' always means . . . 'obey the will of those who claim to speak in the name of god.'"[12] Speaking in the name of reason, the philosophes rein-vested the capacity for speaking the truth in the rational, enlight-ened individual. In this regard, however, their tactic reveals its historical limitations and it is here that Foucault's approach takes a radically different path. Foucault's critique does not rely on faith in reason's capacity for producing truth but brings to our attention the power relations that are activated by the deployment of reason-oriented action: it is in the claim of reason's capacity for determin-ing the course of events that he sees the danger of dogmatism. He shows that the Enlightenment thinkers failed to appreciate the extent to which attempts to universalize values, to attribute to reason or to scientific thought a global and noncontingent validity are power plays, techniques for imposing the rationalizations of specific interests and for legitimizing exclusion and repression. Foucault sees that the idealization of discourse and its grounding in abstractions and transcendental themes produce a regime of truth that makes it possible to ignore the force of other, untheorized and officially unrecognized strategies operative in any given socio-historical context. The latter include the nondiscursive strategies put in place by institutional and disciplinary networks. Since the effects of such unacknowledged power relations do not figure in the official representations of a society's goals and achievements, we are led to believe our existences are governed by the transcendental truths the society espouses, and we forget that "we are forced to produce the truth of power that our society demands, of which it has need, in order to function: we *must* speak the truth. We are constrained or condemned to confess or to discover the truth."[13] The ideology put in place by the Enlightenment was the mecha-nism the new social order needed for producing truths and for elaborating its legitimating alibi.

Foucault's main criticism of the legacy of eighteenth-century thought thus appears to derive from the realization that the failure of the program of enlightened reason is attributable to the process that has made Enlightenment thought the axiological basis for Western civilization. Foucault's theoretical work has sought to un-derscore and explain the discrepancy between the ideals governing our society and the mechanisms that ensure their day-to-day func-tioning. Thus, Foucault proposes that the nineteenth century gave rise to a humanism that effectively masked and validated a socio-economic arrangement whereby forces of social discrimination, domination, and oppression could readily coexist with the official ideology handed down by the French Revolution: "Modern society then, from the nineteenth century up to our own day, has been characterized on the one hand, by a legislation, a discourse, an organisation based on public right, whose principle of articulation is the social body and the delegative status of each citizen; and, on the other hand, by a closely linked grid of disciplinary coercions whose purpose is in fact to assure the cohesion of this same social body." Although the discourse of social and political organization appears to stand opposed to the subterranean and anonymous functioning of disciplinary coercions, the two systems work in tandem: "The powers of modern society are exercised through, on the basis of, and by virtue of, this very heterogeneity between a public right of sovereignty and a polymorphous disciplinary mechanism."[14] Thus from the vantage of a Foucaultian critique, it does appear that "the ideology of the Enlightenment and the disciplinary society are well suited to each other."[15]

A key to Foucault's critical approach, as we have seen, is his innovative theorization of power. Foucault's manner of elucidating the application of power is characteristic of his general strategy of inversion, which serves to uncover the duplicitous nature of strategies of domination in Western society. Such an approach eliminates the alibi of metaphysical themes of human rights and essences and concentrates instead on the material aspects of domination, on the points of application where power produces its real effects. By substituting "the problem of domination for that of sovereignty and obedience" and by conducting an "ascending analysis of power," Foucault demonstrates the collusion of two systems, of the micromechanisms of power inherent in disciplinary practices and the global discourses of right and ethics. In this light, it is not the object of power that holds the key to explaining the system of domination but power itself—its mechanisms, applications, rationales: "It is only if we grasp these techniques of power and demonstrate the economic advantages or political utility that derives from them in a given context for specific reasons, that we can understand how these mechanisms come to be effectively incorporated in a social whole."[16] There is no one scheming or planning to make the system work: that is the secret of its invulnerability and longevity. The system has been functioning so smoothly and efficiently because it has become impossible to distinguish between the justification of power on the one hand and its application on the other, because "the procedures of normalisation come to be ever more constantly engaged in the colonisation of those of law."[17]

From Foucault's perspective, positive principles such as reason and legality imply and are sustained by everything they are not—or unreason and illegality—and it was clear to Foucault that "rational autonomy is itself an empty ideal . . . unless it is exercised critically through the genealogical study of specific, limited historical features of ourselves."[18] As a result, he sought to define the positivity and the sense of all that was familiar and valorized in our culture by bringing to light everything that such a valorization had excluded, banished, silenced. If we consider one of these neglected areas to have been the skeptical, self-questioning, and self-doubting strain in eighteenth-century thought, we can appreciate Foucault's critique as an attempt to restore to the Age of Reason a complexity often covered up by a long tradition of hackneyed and simplistic representations. Thus, for example, Foucault was particularly intrigued by *Le neveu de Rameau,* one of the most memorable of Diderot's fictional creations. He was struck by the uncannily prophetic insights of this text and he singled out the critical importance of Diderot's short masterpiece by placing it in the lineage of the skeptical, non-Cartesian strain of modern thought: "When we consider . . . that the project of Descartes was to tolerate doubt provisionally until truth appeared in the reality of evident ideas, we can see that the non-Cartesian component of modern thought, in its most decisive aspect, does not begin with a discussion of innate ideas, or the incrimination of the ontological argument, but indeed with this text of *Rameau's Nephew,* with this existence it designates in a reversal that was not to be understood before the time of Hölderlin and Hegel."[19] The reversal alluded to by Foucault is the opening the text elaborates toward the otherness of unreason, toward the possibility of a dimension that modern reason will exclude and colonize as madness. For Foucault, Diderot's work already reveals the pattern of thought that was to be fully deployed in the nineteenth century and was to produce a mode of cognition in which humans would become the objects of positive knowledge.

It is a pattern adumbrated by the critique implicit in Diderot's satire. *Rameau's Nephew* brings out a dimension that consistently undermines systematic or "objective" reconstructions of the human experience and the nephew's seemingly incoherent rantings have the effect of disclosing the pretentiousness of reason and its claims to truth. As Rameau observes, whatever knowledge we possess is but an infinitesimal part of the vast symbolic realm of possibilities; consequently, to be able to claim that one knows anything well, one would have to know everything, because, as he points out, "until one knows everything, one knows nothing worth knowing."[20] Once ascertained and disclosed, the limitations of our knowledge and its pretense of systematization bring with them inescapable consequences for the existing system of morality: they produce the realization that distinctions between true and false, good and evil, virtue and vice are only a cover for what really moves things in this world. Superior truths, morality, and the officially recognized values are no more than masks to be worn when the occasion demands it. The fact is that "virtue is praised, but hated. People run away from it, for it is ice-cold and in this world you must keep your feet warm."[21] Virtue, justice, the laws establishing these principles are purely decorative: there are other more effective laws that determine the unfolding of events; to deal effectively with reality, it is these laws that one must respect. Thus it is essential to remember that "in a subject as variable as manners and morals, nothing is absolutely, essentially, universally true or false—unless it be that one must be whatever self-interest requires, good or bad, wise or foolish, decent or ridiculous, honest or vicious."[22] It is this awareness that will put us in tune with the general law of nature to which human existence is subject, to the fundamental principle according to which, "in Nature all species live off one another; in society all classes do the same. We square things up with one another without benefit of the law."[23] It is the law of chaos that reigns, and not the pitifully fragile, approximate, and haphazard fictions humans contrive to explain, represent, justify, and guide their actions. Instead of relying or even contributing to these futile games of codification, "let us accept things then as they are. Let us see what they cost us and what they give us; and let us leave alone the whole that we do not know well enough to either praise or condemn it; and which is perhaps neither good nor evil; even if it is necessary as many honest folk imagine it."[24]

What gives Diderot's insights a decidedly postmodern ring is the conscious rejection of metaphysical abstractions. The editors of Diderot's works have not failed to appreciate this important aspect of his thought. Jacques and Anne-Marie Chouillet have noted that, from our post-Kantian perspective, we might indeed have cause to view *Rameau's Nephew,* together with a number of other works, as part of the same project and place them "in one and the same perspective we could define as a 'critique of practical reason' before the fact, but which would conclude, in a manner contrary to Kant's, by a negation of the categorical imperative."[25] This rejection of a categorical imperative is obviously related to Diderot's materialistic conception of human affairs. Diderot sees human beings developing the meaning for their existence, finding happiness, and being truly themselves only in their relations with their fellows. As Wilda Anderson explains: "In Diderot's relational world picture, where the world of mind is continuous with the world of matter, the private is continuous with the public, because reason is continuous with the passions. Social justice, which is a balancing of the desires of the many, can only really be achieved if the naturalness of self-interest is acknowledged." As a consequence, "self-interest is acknowledged as both inescapable and as the only morally neutral social force."[26] For Diderot, the evidence of a moral existence resides in the material reality of human relations, not in abstract ideals and slogans that only tend to obfuscate reality or divert attention away from the real conditions of existence.

Although such a conceptualization of human relations has obvious affinities with a Marxist approach, Diderot's insights go beyond a strictly materialistic interpretation of human affairs, and his critical view of these could indeed be termed post-Marxist. Diderot saw that the prospects for a progress to be achieved under the guidance of enlightened reason were not at all certain and that the results were likely to disappoint. His skepticism thus places him at the beginning of a distinguished tradition of thinkers who have steadfastly refused to take seriously our civilization's pretense of maturity and high level of accomplishment. It is his understanding of a social existence marked by a two-tiered reality that gives some of his texts a strikingly contemporary ring. He saw that what made the system work was a moral code working in tandem with a Darwinian scheme of survival of the fittest; thus he noted that "not in a single century and not in a single nation have religious opinions served as a basis for national mores."[27] It was clear to him that "supernatural and divine institutions become strengthened and are perpetuated by changing, over time, into civil and national law, and civil and national institutions become consecrated, and degenerate into precepts supernatural and divine."[28] Diderot was thus putting in a nutshell the process that was to characterize the evolution of Western civilization in the following century.

Today a number of critics have come to see the principal task at hand to be the deconstruction of the various transcendental guarantees for sociopolitical processes. Thus, Castoriadis points out that the principle of equality is a cultural "exigency" that is "a creation of *our* history, this segment of history to which we belong." He argues against our customary understanding of axiological causality by noting that "it is absurd to want to found equality upon any particular accepted sense of the term since it is equality which founds us insomuch as we are Europeans." Equality becomes a reality in the context of equal participation, and it is not because certain principles or rules have been proclaimed that they will be realized: "There is only one guarantee for this famous freedom of choice which again has been drummed into our ears for some time now, and this is the active participation in the formation and definition of these rules."[29] The point is, as another critic has put it, that "freedom is not juridical, it is material."[30] Similarly, Foucault finds the best chance for freedom, "not in the mutual obligations of rational agents to obey universal laws, but in our real capacity to change the practices in which we are constituted or constitute ourselves as moral subjects."[31] Such an understanding of a society's capacity for effectuating change independently of the will of rational humans, well intentioned though they might be, has brought about a new and radically skeptical approach to the notion of change.

Little by little, and in spite of the best efforts of intellectuals striving to fulfill the promise implicit in the project of modernity, the reassuring myths of rationally controllable change and of a foreseeable unified destiny have dissipated; the phenomenon of change has become overwhelming, uncontrollable, and—what is more, global: "For the first time in human history, all societies are *all together* undergoing multiple and cumulative transformations; also for the first time, the most enterprising societies are overwhelmed by the number, the speed, and the incidence of changes they generate—so that Marx's famous formula could well be inverted: it is much less a question of changing them than of understanding them, in order to acquire the capacity for governing their movement."[32] In the face of this realization, the strategy of the postmodern critics has consisted of two major modifications of traditional approaches to the question of change. One is to downplay the importance of the intellectual and to reject the claim that he or she can effectively and actively affect the march of events or the direction of history. Secondly, postmodern thinkers find that the focus, scope, and very nature of intellectual activity have to change. Foucault believed, for example, that we are still trapped in a limited and limiting mode of thought that keeps us running in circles over the same territory and the same issues; he therefore found that "we must free ourselves from the sacralization of the social as the only reality and stop regarding as superfluous something so essential in human life and in human relations as thought." To counter these tendencies ingrained in our approach to the world of intellect, Foucault suggested we recognize that "thought exists independently of systems and structures of discourse. It is something that is often hidden, but which always animates everyday behavior."[33] By granting thought an autonomous existence that is no longer subject to the decrees of will, Foucault demolished the commonsensical link between knowledge and reality that had informed all of modernity: "I know very well, and I think I knew it from the moment when I was a child," Foucault observed, "that knowledge can do nothing for transforming the world. Maybe I am wrong. And I am sure I am wrong from a theoretical point of view for I know very well that knowledge has transformed the world."[34] The knowledge that transforms the world is what becomes available to us after the fact, but the changes taking place are due to causes that will only be understood by generations following ours—and imperfectly, even then.

It is hardly possible, therefore, to elaborate self-confident rationales of progress or perfectibility to guide our actions, and it becomes more and more difficult to rely on familiar ways of think-ing about ourselves, our past, and our aspirations; this leads us to recognize the main purpose of criticism, which "is a matter of flushing out that thought and trying to change it: to show that things are not as self-evident as one believed, to see that what is accepted as self-evident will no longer be accepted as such. Practic-ing criticism is a matter of making facile gestures difficult."[35] Such an approach obviously fails to offer the promise of easy, clear-cut solutions. Foucault's example, for one, "offers no ideological plot to diminish the agony of human choice confronted with events that remind men that human time has the form of a history and not of an evolution."[36] Although such an outlook acknowledges the fail-ure of the Enlightenment's sociopolitical project, it also attests to the continuing influence of the ideas constituting the political and ethical force of Enlightenment thought. It is a realization that requires that we raise all over again the issues relating to the pur-pose and rationality of human society and that we question once more the ties between politics and philosophy, ideas and existence. The relation between the old ideals and the human condition has undergone an evident transformation; this realization does not diminish the importance of thought or deny its effect on the world: it only calls for a new—or, to put it more precisely—for a renewed ethos of enlightened commitment. Foucault, again, has put it quite succinctly: "The thread that may connect us with the Enlighten-ment is not faithfulness to doctrinal elements, but rather the perma-nent reactivation of an attitude—that is, of a philosophical ethos that could be described as a permanent critique of our historical era."[37] It is not reality that is to be critiqued in a vain attempt at influencing the course of human affairs, but the thought and the thinking processes that represent this reality for us.

The questioning that postmodern theorizing promotes lets us discover that the process of decentering the notion of "man" from the paranoid assumption that it is the source and ultimate goal of all activity in the universe has been unfolding for some time. Whence the radical ambiguity of the postmodern critique of the Enlighten-ment: as it critically examines the legacy, it is drawn to the source in which it recognizes itself. Because this questioning recognizes itself as an integral part of the legacy of the Enlightenment, it is also impelled to reconsider the Enlightenment itself. As it does this, it has an opportunity to demonstrate, not only that our civilization has failed to complete the project of the Enlightenment—something that is obvious to many—but that it never really had a chance—until now, perhaps, when the illusion of establishing mastery over the real has been fully disclosed. The problematization of the Enlightenment has brought out the emptiness of claims to fuse transcendental with empirical thought, or to reconcile universal and totalizing themes with the temporality of their expression. However, in this regard at least, postmodern thought has not uncovered anything that the Age of Enlightenment, in its more lucid moments, did not already know.

CHAPTER 6

CANDIDE'S GARDEN REVISITED: THE POSTMODERN VIEW

Candide's recommendation that we cultivate our garden has by now served in countless ways to illustrate certain aspects of Voltaire's philosophy as well as a particular ethos of the Age of Enlightenment. It is not my intention to review the many interpretations or to survey the controversy in order to produce a definitive explanation for the conclusion of Voltaire's famous conte. Anyone interested in the history of the debate will find it recounted in the introduction written for the volume on *Candide* in the Modern Language Association's series "Approaches to Teaching World Literature."[1] Renée Waldinger's overview of the debate gives us a good idea of the rich variety of points of view on this question. This diversity also suggests that an eventual consensus is most unlikely. What recommends Candide's famous statement to our attention is the curious new life it appears to have acquired of late. In the context of the postmodern debates surrounding the whole notion of the Enlightenment and of its legacy in particular, the metaphor of the garden can be taken as a paradigm for what is emerging as a central theme in postmodernist approaches. A reconsideration of Candide's assertion can thus be doubly helpful today: first, it gives us an occasion to appreciate the relevance of Voltaire to our age by making us focus on one aspect that gives his thought a special resonance for our time. Second, it can help us gain a more precise understanding of what is at issue in the discussions on and around the postmodern critical stance toward the Enlightenment.

We saw in the preceding chapter that postmodern critiques of modernity are inevitably characterized by an ever-present tension between the desire to discredit modernity and the realization that they cannot claim to transcend modernity without being co-opted by it; they are also debilitated by the suspicion that they may very well owe their shape and impulses to modernity itself. This dilemma marks equally the present-day critical reevaluations of Enlightenment, which operate between the need to understand the deficiencies of Enlightenment philosophy and the obligation to recognize their indebtedness to it. This is "the lesson of postmodernism's complex relation to modernism: its retention of modernism's initial oppositional impulses, both ideological and aesthetic, and its equally strong rejection of its founding notion of formalist autonomy."[2]

One of the principal concerns of the philosophes, as we well know, was the eradication of superstition and the disclosure of the collusion between revealed knowledge and secular power. Their critique very effectively demonstrated the ruse of strategies of domination; they saw that "the insistence of dogmatists that their 'truths' have come by revelation—as it were to compensate for their insufficiency as evidence—implies the unwarrantable postulate of a knowledge independent of observation." And they understood quite clearly that "the motive behind the insistence is always the desire of those claiming a revelation to impose themselves as depositaries of it."[3] We now realize, and postmodern criticism has been particularly insistent on this point, that modernity reproduced the very tactic it had sought to discredit. While doing away with the previous ground for truthful discourse—the authority of God—the philosophes established another transcendental authority—that of reason. By replacing God with an equally transcendent and unimpeachable concept, the Enlightenment set in place a mechanism that could again be exploited by those with the authority to impose truth—an authority derived not from empirically verifiable evidence but implying a reliance on a knowledge freed from the contingency of its socioeconomic and historical context.

The mechanism of truth remained the same, however: "Whether this ordering force is a divine being or only a human being who appears as God's representative or successor is not crucial. The essential point is rather the gesture of domination and appropriation that arises from this situation."[4] The original model for this tactic is of course to be found in Descartes, "who nominates human beings as 'maîtres et possesseurs de la nature' " and who effectuated the elision that gave the rational project its supreme confidence in itself; it was, consequently, "a project which affirms that no part of the social condition is beyond analysis, and thus that the orderly workings of social power can be guaranteed through the development and application of knowledge. This project enshrines a denial of otherness, of difference. It is, effectively, *the* absolutist project, unconsciously designed along lines of complete domination."[5] The domination was made effective once the ideology of the Enlightenment was integrated within the socioeconomic system. Under the cover of universal values authorized by reason, it was the reason of a specific race, gender, and social class that was smuggled in. The collusion between reason and universals gave Western bourgeois thought the will and the prerogative to colonize—to impose its value system in the name of principles that were deemed self-evident and therefore indisputable.

The project of modernity was therefore debilitated from the start by a tautological process that was implicit in its self-assertiveness. This circularity still manifests itself in several regards. First, the very notion of the modern is fundamentally flawed, as a number of critics have observed. Indeed, it is an absurd concept because it is based on the premise of its own endless, never-changing mode of being; ironically, because it cannot, by definition, be overcome, the notion of the modern ends up negating progress and enshrining the status quo; as Cornelius Castoriadis sees it, "The term 'modern' expresses a profoundly auto (or ego-) centric attitude. The proclamation 'we are the moderns' tends to cancel any true ulterior development." Moreover, argues Castoriadis, the term is self-contradictory and "only makes sense on the absurd hypothesis that the period that has proclaimed itself modern will last forever and that future will only be a prolonged present."[6] The recent and well publicized article by Francis Fukuyama announcing the end of history and the triumph of the Western sociopolitical model could thus be seen as an attempt to ratify this absurdity and to demonstrate the truth of the redundancy which consists of asserting that modernity is indeed what it is—forever modern and thus unimpeachable.[7]

The Enlightenment saw the future of humanity in terms of a unified history and a progress made possible by the irresistible advancement of knowledge. However, in the attempt to establish its unchallengeable status of ever-newness, modernity was in fact negating history by pretending to be able to escape from the effects of the past; this is a critique elaborated by Gadamer. According to him, the error of the Enlightenment "was to discredit 'prejudices' and to propose an ideal of understanding which requires that one transcend one's present and free oneself from one's insertion into history."[8] In order to do this Enlightenment thought had to posit a supreme reason that freed it from the weight of past ignorance. .

At the same time, such a mode of thought fell victim to a prejudice that was inherent in its self-confident procedure, one made legitimate by an axiomatic reference to the principle of universal reason. Thus, while Enlightenment thought inaugurated freedom of inquiry and opened up all areas of thought to exhaustive investigation, it left out one crucial element, namely, the investigator's own authority to investigate. As a consequence of this elision, the eighteenth-century thinker was authorized to proceed on the basis of an unshakable trust in the righteousness and rational potential of his critical project; it was a "belief that the progress of inquiry will yield the improvement of humankind and society; and confidence in the emancipatory power of rational critique."[9] The abstraction of human existence made possible by this formulation has had a debilitating effect on the critical potential of modernity. This was already understood by the philosophers of the Frankfurt School; Horkheimer notes that "the basic ideals and concepts of rationalist metaphysics were rooted in the concept of the universally human, of mankind, and their formalization implies that they have been severed from their human content."[10]

By imposing its logic and order as expressions of the most advanced, progressive, reformist—even revolutionary—thought, modernity was able to internalize mechanisms of reform and resistance as part of a strategy for self-preservation. Postmodern critics have been particularly interested in disclosing "the extent to which modernism and the avantgarde as forms of an adversary culture were nevertheless conceptually and practically bound up with capitalist modernization and/or with communist vangardism, that modernization's twin brother."[11] Both the liberal and Marxist critical traditions can thus be analyzed in terms of a common origin since they are both "rooted in the Enlightenment project of social, cultural, and political rationality." What they both have in common is a reliance on "propositions about the *universality* of that project—as a social logic through which the world ought to transform itself in the image of Western men. Western Enlightenment philosophy thereby creates a world of universals in order to imagine itself as universal for the rest of the world."[12]

Although feminist critics are understandably suspicious of certain aspects of postmodernism, they have found useful a critical approach that uncovers the specific interests served by a promulgation of humanistic themes and have adopted strategies generally associated with postmodernist thinking to bring out the subtle ways in which the reigning rationality manages to occlude or downplay the capacity social relations have for imposing domination and exclusion. As a consequence, feminists share with postmodernist critics a generally suspicious attitude toward values promoted by various claims of universal applicability. Even the concept of democracy, as Carol Pateman demonstrates, has its source in a strategy that aimed to exclude women:

> The idea of universal citizenship is especially modern, and necessarily depends on the emergence of the view that all individuals are born free and equal, or are naturally free and equal to each other. No individual is naturally subordinate to another, and all must thus have public standing as citizens, that upholds their self-governing status. Individual freedom and equality also entails that government can arise only through agreement or consent. We are all taught that the "individual" is a universal category that applies to anyone or everyone, but this is not the case. "The individual" is a man.[13]

Man was indeed the central element and the unquestioned referent of modernity's strategy to establish a ground for its system of values. This attempt to legitimate its own limitations as the foundation for its axiological system has given modernity its tautological pattern. Foucault described it as an "analytic of finitude"; the political scientist William Connolly characterizes it as an "aspiration to articulate the container into which its own discourse has been poured."[14] It could be argued that this self-referentiality was bound to turn critical and become self-debilitating. It has apparently given way to a postmodern lucidity whose function has been to disclose modernity's contradictions, inconsistencies, and tautologies. Accordingly, a postmodern critical perspective serves to bring out the ingenuousness of many of modernity's procedures by disclosing the contradictions in their self-referential ways of ethical valorization. In light of this critique, "what appears anomalous is the modern tendency, which is inherited from Kant, to believe in the narrative of Enlightenment and to hold paradoxically the two premises, namely that social progress must accompany the growth of knowledge, and that knowledge is logically independent of the social conditions of its acquisition and communication."[15] This perspective also shows that the possibility of placing knowledge outside the conditions that produced it—a privilege modernity arrogated for itself from the start—constitutes a mechanism that is fundamental to the contemporary technocratic arrangement. Thus, it is evident that attempts to rationalize society in order to make it transparent to the scientific, technical mind are still driven by a desire to fulfill the telos of an Enlightenment-oriented ideology.

The technological ideal has given rise, for example, to the "heroic expert," the incarnation of the dominant instrumental ethic, which is also a dominant masculinist ethic, as a number of feminists have argued. Irene Diamond, a leading proponent of ecofeminism, studies the evolution of systems of microcontrol in which the role of heroic experts is to cover up the dysfunctional aspects of the socioeconomic scheme. She makes the rather shocking point that "in an economy built upon a growing trade in toxic materials, drugs, and radiation, babies are the best "canaries" we have—that pregnancy can provide a warning much like the canary did for coal miners. Clusters of infertility, miscarriages, contaminated breast milk, and birth defects can be important signals." The application of various technologies can help hide the signals and divert public attention away from the socioeconomic conditions that produce the symptoms by drawing it to techniques designed to alleviate them. In this manner, the conditions can remain unchallenged and social and political problems are turned into concerns for science. As a result, concludes Diamond, "the power of heroic experts is extended, the toxicities of late capitalism persist, and the poisoning of the Earth can continue."[16] This habit of using technical solutions to cover up the dysfunctional aspects of society has become a favorite tactic of certain kinds of politicians who call for more prisons and more frequent executions to solve the drug crisis, for example. It has been aptly characterized as a "compulsion to transform the misery of society into sickness of nature." In addition, the heroization of technical intervention also produces a distorted notion of change, of its potential and causes. Thus, the idea of a hero, as Bernauer notes, "has served as a device to explain change apart from the millions of unknowns who are responsible for that change."[17]

The result of the heroization of technical expertise, of the relentless rationalization of the world, has produced an awareness of the ineptitude of a technocratic rationality—a situation whose irony Voltaire would certainly have found delectable. The impotence of reason, in turn, can be explained by a failure to understand that by itself, as a noncontingent abstract ideal, reason could not guarantee its own application—since it could only serve as an alibi, a transcendental reference. A reliance on an abstract ideal is only an invitation to disaster, as Voltaire demonstrated in his witty tales. Pierre Bayle, an influential philosophical predecessor of Voltaire, observed that, in an ideal world, humans would be expected to act according to their official convictions; this was evidently—and unfortunately—not the case in our world and he was led to conclude that man "almost never acts in accordance with his principles."[18] Camus echoed this belief two and a half centuries later when he observed that "law can reign in fact, in so far as it is the law of universal reason. But it never is, and it loses its justification if man is not naturally good. A day comes when ideology conflicts with psychology."[19] It is in this skeptical tradition that we can situate Foucault's conviction that "reason did not necessarily produce rationality; on the contrary, the very project of rational control, while other social relations remained unchanged, produced unreason."[20] This realization sums up the general attitude implicit in postmodern criticism, which has recognized that the real is not directly accessible to rational thought and only the subterfuge of transcendental themes could keep us in that illusion.

The connection between theory and practice, thought and reality, philosophy and politics has, by now, been irreparably broken. Reason, especially in its manipulative instrumental version, can no longer be taken as the sufficient force for creating the perfect society. This is because society, as Castoriadis has pointed out, "is a form of self-creation." Characteristically, it is "a self-instituting which is occulted from itself" and which is carried out by dint of "the representation of a source of the instituting of society which can only be found *outside* this society: among the gods, in God, among the ancestors, in the laws of Nature, in the laws of Reason, in the laws of History."[21]

Just like Candide in his garden, the postmodern critic has become distrustful of abstract philosophy and adopts a more modest, practical approach: "At the 'end of philosophy' as theoretical critique, we encounter a refiguration of rationality as *praxial* critique. Critique is resituated within the dynamics of our sociohistorical engagements. . . . Critique becomes a communicative project, a praxis that finds its resources in the dialogic transactions and institutional forms that make up the fabric of our historical existence."[22] With the notable exception of Jean-Jacques Rousseau, Enlightenment thinkers were not so much concerned with producing recipes for progress as with questioning entrenched beliefs and attacking abuses: "The leaders of the 'High Enlightenment' were not primarily trading in down-to-earth political nostrums; they were more concerned with making palpable hits with their criticism, and with a far more sweeping and imaginative attempt to create a new, more humane, more scientific understanding of man as a social and natural being. They were less concerned with blueprints than with analysis, less with conclusions than with questions."[23] Postmodern critics have modified this program by abandoning themes of humanistic and scientific pretense but have retained its basic spirit. They recognize the futility of founding a politically correct stance, of reconciling the political project with the epistemological requirements of objective thought. Such a realization gives the postmodernist an important advantage: "Once we acknowledge that there is no necessary relation between these two aspects, we are in the position of being able to defend the political project while abandoning the notion that it must be based on a specific form of rationality."[24] In fact, the removal of foundations does not take away anything that is real or tangible—it only removes the imaginary alibi. And the lack of founding truths makes the project less likely to be exploited by those who would claim to be depositaries of revealed truths.

Moreover, the loss of foundations does not necessarily entail the abandoning of all values and principles, contrary to what many critics of postmodernism have claimed. It is the symbolic ascendancy of a community and not alleged theoretical foundations that provides the incentive and models for ethical behavior: "It is always possible to distinguish between the just and the unjust, the legitimate and the illegitimate, but this can be done from within a given tradition, with the help of standards that this tradition provides."[25] Max Horkheimer offers us a very useful reminder in this regard: "Thought is faithful to itself largely through being ready to contradict itself, while preserving, as inherent elements of truth, the memory of the process by which it was reached."[26] The postmodern approach accepts therefore that it cannot separate itself from the complex and messy story of its own development. But it has lost the comforting privilege of justifications that can be placed outside and above the concrete experience of individuals immersed in the context of their community. From this arises the understanding that remedies to social problems can no longer be dictated by an elite of party intellectuals, for example. As Foucault points out, an effective solution to problems concerning the daily life of individuals is most likely to be found in a fundamentally democratic process, because "it takes years, decades of work carried out at the grassroots level with the people directly involved; and the right to speech and political imagination must be returned to them."[27]

The focus of critical inquiry has shifted today from imaginary slogans to the symbolic world of social interaction and cultural representation. As a result, "once life is seen neither as an unfolding intentionality nor as an external chain of causation, living, both individual and collective, acquires the connotation of a struggle or *agon,* of an ongoing creative (though not willful) praxis."[28] What such a struggle involves, then, is the cultivation of "a 'practical reason,' a region not characterized by apodictic statements, where the reasonable prevails over the demonstrable."[29] The intellectual's pretensions are reduced, accordingly, to a more modest level. They consist, as Foucault put it, of doing the work of the specific intellectual, of dealing with the concrete problems pertaining to one's intellectual specialty. This work no longer enjoys the guarantee offered by a transcendental reason, or a destiny, or a nature that will ensure humanity's survival in the face of the greed, cruelty, and stupidity of humans. On the other hand, it is likely to be more effective because it accepts a condition Lyotard has brought to our attention; as Gayle Ormiston puts it, it is "the necessity of recognizing that in whatever domain, whatever field of inquiry, in whatever phrasic network, one is without a rule, one already judges without criteria. That is to say, one is without recourse to a meta-language, a *grand récit*."[30] This awareness does not diminish the need for responsibility, for deciding a course of action, and for facing a problem of evil that remains just as acute in our time as it was for Voltaire; indeed, this problem can be taken to be one of the clearest sources of postmodern anguish and skepticism. Following Adorno, Lyotard considers "Auschwitz" to represent that which invalidates any realistic claim of progress in the human condition. He asks: "What sort of thought would be capable of lifting up, in the sense of *aufheben,* 'Auschwitz' by placing it in a general, empirical and even speculative process, aimed at universal emancipation?"[31] It is a question that can have no answer, yet has to be asked.

Thus the modest recommendation offered at the conclusion of Voltaire's philosophical tale seems to fit quite nicely the mood of our own age. Which means that we are rediscovering something that Voltaire believed in profoundly: that the recourse to abstract systems and metaphysical explanations is the way to delusion and catastrophe; and that constant vigilance, critical attention, and skepticism are still the best weapons for confronting the reality of the human condition.

It is not a stance that is either easy or comfortable to maintain, contrary to what Barthes implies when he characterizes Voltaire as "the last of the happy writers." As Patrick Henry has shown, Barthes simply failed to appreciate the complexity and ambiguity of Voltaire's thought and was particularly insensitive to the depth and intricacy of the *contes philosophiques.* The only way, Henry points out, "one can draw a line from Voltaire to M. Homais is to read Voltaire as M. Homais would have done. One has to read Voltaire without any imagination in order to 'prove' that he does not have any." Indeed, what stands out in Barthes's reading of Voltaire is a romantic leftism that takes existential anguish for a sign of intellectual superiority. Moreover, it is not Voltaire's historical awareness but the teleological view espoused by Barthes that appears limiting today:

> To equate Voltaire's lack of system with anti-intellectualism, as Barthes does, is a grave error. It is precisely because Voltaire believed in history as a *devenir,* the end of which could not be ascertained in advance, rather than as an *être,* that he refused to close himself up in any system. In a special sense, this makes him a greater champion of the intelligence than the system makers, for he would not imprison his mind with slavish adherence to a particular theory or abstraction, believing, as he did, that all systems, theories, and abstractions ultimately contradict factual reality to which he wanted to remain faithful. [32]

The world was not simple for Voltaire, who was "caught in a dilemma which has never ceased to torment post-Enlightenment man." The quandary is made especially explicit in *Candide,* a tale that "expresses in permanent form the emotion of the agnostic who cannot believe in the senselessness of the universe and yet cannot make sense of it."[33] Although Voltaire despaired sometimes on witnessing the absurdity and ferocity of which humans are capable, his resolve to combat ignorance and superstition never wavered. The dilemma never immobilized Voltaire, it simply made him less prone than others to entertain hopes predicated on the lure of systematicity.

CHAPTER 7

THE POLITICS OF
A POSTMODERN CRITIQUE

MICHEL FOUCAULT POINTS out in *The Order of Things* that "knowl-edge of man, unlike the sciences of nature, is always linked, even in its vaguest form, to ethics and politics." It could well be argued that contemporary forms of literary and cultural criticism as they have evolved in the wake of poststructuralism are very much predicated on this understanding. Yet this critical practice has also been shaped by the realization that the hope of securing logical and causal ties between knowledge, ethics, and politics is ultimately a vain one. It is this very impossibility of theorizing morality, of mooring one's critical *engagement* to a universal value system, that has led to an increasing emphasis on praxis, to the advocacy of a postmodern practice of criticism—one that no longer seeks to justify itself in terms of all-encompassing rationales. The postmodern critic has seen through the illusions fostered by such rationales and accepts the intrusion of the ineffable, of an imponderable and insuperable otherness in his or her activity.

At the same time, the intellectual lucidity achieved by this crit-ical practice has been seemingly bought at the cost of political ineffectiveness; the dilemma is due to criticism's adversarial stance vis-à-vis the general ethos of individual responsibility still holding sway in our society, a stance that places its practitioners in a radi-cally alienated position with regard to its power brokers. Some see this condition as a fundamental characteristic of the civilization of modernity: "The unique aspect of modernity, that which makes it a barbarism of a type not seen before, is precisely its ability to exist as a society deprived of all culture and to subsist independently of the latter."[1] Similarly, George F. Kennan has analyzed the situation as a tragic development in the history of the United States:

> I view the United States of these last years of the 20th century as essentially a tragic country, endowed with magnificent natural resources which it is rapidly wasting and exhausting, and with an intellectual and artistic intelligentsia of great talent and originality of which the dominant political forces of the country have little understanding or regard. Its voice is normally silenced or outshouted by the commercial media. It is probably condemned to remain indefinitely, like the Russian intelligentsia in the 19th century, a helpless spectator of the disturbing course of a nation's life.[2]

Today's humanists are likely to experience an anxiety and frustration that is attributable precisely to such a feeling of irrelevance in a society where the concerns informing humanities are increasingly overshadowed by those shaping the thinking of the decision makers. But the growing rift can also be taken as a sign of the gradual disintegration of modernity—and of modern notions of the political in particular. Political leaders, by and large, still operate in terms of the obsolescent modernistic model for human behavior fashioned by commonsensical and religious notions of individual autonomy and responsibility that stand in marked contrast with the view that has become a commonplace in contemporary critical theory, namely, that "the functions men exercise and the norms which determine them, the conflicts men develop and the rules which regulate them, the significations men give and the linguistic systems which govern them are largely unthought."[3] Thus, although this aspect of our experience remains largely unarticulated, experience itself increasingly imposes its impressions in ways that commonsensical notions are no longer able to explain.

The critical approaches being elaborated in the context of the postmodern condition can be considered attempts to come to grips with this condition, as ways of exploring and exploiting the freedom of inquiry made possible by the dissolution of the metaphysical themes that used to hold guidelines for interpreting reality in place. It is the distance between the effects of the Other and our experience of these effects that allows for freedom; this discrepancy can be investigated and expanded by critical practices aimed at the processes of symbolization constituting the individual's sociocultural experience. The realm of the social is of course the space of the political, which, in a democratic system, can be seen as made up "of the choices and decisions that constitute the forms of reduction of complexity that permit the social system to be maintained."[4] One important aim of a postmodern critical activity has been to re-introduce a complexity that does justice to the ongoing negotiations and decisions constituting what passes for the democratic process in our society. The function of cultural and literary criticism is thus specified as the search for the unthought norms and rules that govern the thinking of a community; it seeks to define the space where the play of language impinges on the application of power and on the interaction of individualized desires. In this regard, a postmodern approach reveals that the claim to promote objective or value-free knowledge for the benefit of humankind hides a limited and strictly circumscribed purpose working to benefit the unavowed causes of specific interests. The official subject in such cases is an alibi, a useful fiction for avoiding situations that are either too complex or too compromising to face.

Those who subscribe to the metaphysical guarantees of the old order tend to resist attempts at exposing this reality; they issue calls for a return to a prelapsarian practice of the humanities and hold the new theoretical approaches responsible for the decline of cultural and educational standards. At the Madison Center—the conservative think tank founded by William Bennett and Allan Bloom—a recent conference on "Restoring American Education" identified the obstacle in the way of the desired restoration as certain intellectual trends that could be considered "dominant in many humanities fields" and that include "poststructuralism, postmodernism, deconstruction, feminism, black studies, and efforts to broaden the curriculum to include non-Western perspectives."[5] The condemnation of these trends is based on the claim that they threaten the very foundations of society by promoting an abandonment of intellectual standards. To preserve this distinction between the old values and attempts to subvert them, the defenders of the traditional order have found it necessary to indict critiques of Western thought by denouncing them as strategic components of an insidious campaign to relativize all values and all notions of objective truth.

In addition to impugning the proponents of relativism on moral grounds, the defenders of objectivism also propose an epistemological argument they consider well-nigh irrefutable:

> It has always been the dilemma of relativist eclectic and pluralist positions that they are constrained to exempt themselves from those strictures and limitations with which they wish to surround every other position—or style. For relativism is never able to turn back on itself and view itself *relatively*. No relativist will ever proclaim his own position as one option among many. And by subsuming all other positions, relativism is doomed to re-establish itself on the pedestal of the very authoritarianism, or totalitarianism, which it was its *raison d'être* to challenge.[6]

The logic of the argument, although at first sight impeccable, is flawed in several regards; in the first place, to define relativism as a "position" is already to formulate the argument in terms of objectivist criteria, of a logic of "truths." What the objectivist position fails to recognize is that the opponent it construes is its own mirror image; it therefore ignores the fact of its own dogmatism. The objectivists are willing to pursue the argument only in terms of the principles defining their own logic, which is predicated on the assumption that there is an ascertainable reality and a truth that preexist their elaboration in discourse. For postmodern critics, the assumption to be demonstrated is *not* the relativity or contingency of values, beliefs, and truths but the immutability and permanence of the alleged ground on which these are founded.

What appears anomalous, aberrant, from a postmodern vantage, is the obstinacy with which objectivists cling to designations "true" and "valid." This propensity for marshaling apodictic evidence is illustrated by the objectivists' refusal to see that the force of their own persuasions and arguments stems less from some fundamental and universal logic than from an entrenched authority legitimized by tradition, processes of naturalization, ideological commitments, and economic interests; of course, such a refusal only brings the attention of cultural critics to the pragmatic motives behind it. Conversely, the axiological convictions of the promoters of traditional conceptions of knowledge prevent them from seeing the extent to which their own intervention is political; the narrowness of their definition of the political helps them evade what is becoming increasingly obvious, that what they seek to prevent is the revelation of the political involvement of all knowledge. It is obviously useful to dissimulate the political implications of such a strategy by claiming to base one's convictions on a procedure that is epistemologically unimpeachable. But the tactic is becoming transparent:

> When someone or some group of people insist(s) on the *objective* necessity or propriety of their own social, political, or moral judgments and actions, and deny the *contingency* of the conditions and perspective from which those judgments and actions proceed, it must be—and always is—a move to assign dominant status to the *particular* conditions and perspectives that happen to be relevant to or favored by that person, group, or class; it must be—and always is— simultaneously a move to deny the existence and relevance, and to suppress the claims, of *other* conditions and perspectives.[7]

The most effective way to deny the political implications of any strategy that attempts to impose truth in the name of intangible transcendental themes is to maintain a clear separation between the realm of political and scholarly activities and to construe practices that are critical of established axiological systems as an unwarranted politicization of issues that ought to remain within the purview of dispassionate inquiry: to view them, in other words, as constituting a betrayal of the humanist's responsibilities. For the defenders of conservative values, the suspicion of political motives is a damning accusation; the comments made by the editor of the *New Criterion* ring with a characteristically ominous tone: "We all know—and certainly our enemies know—that the assault on the arts and the humanities . . . is, above all, a political assault—an attempt on the part of the radical Left first to discredit and then to do away with what in our most exalted artistic and humanistic traditions may be seen to offer resistance, either directly or by implication, to the total politicization of culture and life."[8]

The notion that "culture and life" can be kept unpoliticized stems from a worldview that makes it not only possible but imperative to separate the cultural from the political. Sidney Hook once provided a distinction that could be considered classical. In his address to the 1968 meeting of the Modern Language Association, he drew a sharp distinction between two roles a university professor is expected to assume: those of citizen and of scholar. Accordingly, "as a citizen he is inescapably limited by duties to the nation that bestows citizenship upon him, but as a scholar he is a citizen of the world." The noblest role is that of scholar, because "in serving truth, one *is* serving all mankind." This service is then the proper function of the scholar and, as a consequence, it stands to reason that the scholar's institution, the university, "must not take sides in the clash of social goals." Furthermore, according to Hook, such a refusal to take sides cannot in itself be deemed political and "to argue . . . that the refusal of a university or professional association to take a position on a political issue is, in virtue of that very refusal, taking a political position is completely without merit."[9]

Twenty years later, we find Hook reiterating this conviction in an article published posthumously in the *National Review:* "In the study of the humanities, we can legitimately inquire into the influence of political decisions in the past on the ideals and models conceived to represent the best and most enduring in art and literature. But that is quite different from selecting readings in a course or teaching them in order to reshape the politics of the present or future." The latter course of action is not legitimate because it belongs to a sphere of activity which is "the public and legislative forum, not the institutions for the dissemination of wisdom, let alone the curriculum of the humanities." To confuse the two is to relativize the notion of truth and, Hook adds, "to hold that objectivity is a myth is tantamount to denying the distinction between fiction and history, guilt and innocence, in relation to the admitted evidence."[10] Of course, what Hook doesn't point out is that he and others who share his views are mostly concerned with remaining in control of the process that determines what evidence will be judged admissible. The attitude is a revealing example of what Barbara Herrnstein Smith identifies as "a fundamental principle of all cognitive process—namely the will to epistemic self-maintenance—a *conservatism* that may be even deeper than that of politics or, in the literal sense, economic self-interest."[11] Distinctions between what is legitimately political and what is not are obviously made to serve the purposes of those who have the power to make those distinctions and are afraid of losing it. They serve to eliminate certain kinds of arguments and inquiries and to preserve the officially sanctioned political realm from being contaminated by undue skepticism.

There is, in our culture, a long tradition of intellectual and academic pursuits unfettered by political considerations. Richard Ohmann finds that the occlusion of the political involvement of culture is made possible by "the mesmeric power still carried by the idea that criticism, or English, or the great books, or the humanities, or culture, can somehow stand off from the clash of purposes and interests, and serve some higher purpose of its own in a politically neutral way." This Arnoldian theme is necessary to impart the conviction that the moral is the realm of individual responsibility, to make individuals believe they are free of hegemonic influences, and to ensure that "the personal and political habits that go with [the hegemony of a class] feel like choices *we make*."[12] The class of intellectuals is very important in this regard: it helps mediate the relations between the decision makers and the general population, between the powerful and the dominated. Today, however, the discourse of mediation seems to be rapidly losing its powers of conviction and is giving way to a perspective that allows for the possibility of apprehending the norms and presuppositions that regulate life in society, without the benefit of metaphysical blinders.

The lucidity offered by contemporary critical perspectives has led first to the realization that *in practice* things have not worked out according to theory, especially in the case of our most cherished ideals—those we have inherited from the Enlightenment. The notion of democracy itself is being reexamined today and the uses to which the concept of democracy are put are being brought into question. Claude Lefort points out, for example, that the institution of democracy was made possible by the void created following the removal of the figure that occupied the seat of authority. Consequently, he proposes we see democracy as a system with no *body* and with no centrally localizable place or focus of authority. At most, it has representative figures, but these, as we all know, owe their authority to the will of the people. This will, in turn, is mainly characterized by its instability because it is, after all, the will of a tenuous majority; furthermore, it usually is nothing more than a momentary coalescence of interests. The true nature of a democracy is thus to be realized in the process that characterizes its operation: it is an interminable series of collective negotiations and decisions carried out in a society no longer dominated by themes of essences or the ontological alibis that used to legitimate manifestations of power.[13]

In a similar manner, the concepts of state and state power are losing their substance and specificity. Up until now, the state had also operated on the model of the autonomous individual and had accordingly been conceptualized as a willful, responsible, and responsive—sometimes threatening, sometimes solicitous—manager of its citizen's lives. But here also theory fails to convince. As David Couzens Hoy points out, "A central characteristic of postmodern thinkers is that when the question is one about social theory and social science, they are incredulous about the idea of holding state power rationally accountable for a complex modern society."[14] The French philosopher Jacques Donzelot notes that "in the last twenty years, in France, we have gone from a condemnation of the evils caused by the alleged almightiness of the State to an avowed suspicion of its impotence."[15] The state is manifestly becoming less and less effective in a world where essences are no longer operative as concepts: in the face of state-sponsored rationality, the world increasingly appears to operate according to its own rules.

As the traditional concepts used for explaining and legitimizing a society lose their cogency, it becomes obvious that knowledge, especially in a technocratic society run by experts wielding a highly specialized knowledge, is not separable from the general metaphysical presuppositions of Western culture. The logic and rationality of technology is only a kind of rhetoric and the pretense of the autonomous, self-legislating and self-legitimating intellectual or scientist simply occludes the lack of moral authority that characterizes the postmodern condition. The essence of technology, we are beginning to learn, is metaphysical; the ruling system of values is a lack of values: it is exchange value—a general equivalency that ensures the permanence of the existing hierarchies of power in society because the driving force is an unofficial yet most effective motivator—it is the profit motive. The logic of exchange value has absorbed that of use value, the quantifiable has replaced the metaphysical notions of the authentic, the original, the proper. As a result, rationality is no longer evident in the self-regulating mechanisms of late capitalism. Thus, as Ohmann points out, "the main irrationality of capitalism—that socially produced wealth is privately allocated, and so allocated by the sole criterion of profitability"—finds itself reproduced in a fundamental contradiction that marks our institutions of education as well as our political system. Simply put, "liberal values are necessary to the maintenance of advanced capitalism, yet advanced capitalism prevents their fulfillment." The term *free market,* for example, is "without a referent in the real world"; it therefore needs a context of an ideological discourse of freedom and equality to maintain its credibility and legitimacy. The force of culture is therefore mobilized to advance the economic ends of the ruling sphere of interests; under the cloak of a liberal ideology, the effect of this strategy is "to advance the freedom of large corporations in making markets and people unfree."[16] This is why culture has a fundamentally political role to play, why cultural and educational institutions are suffused with politics; this has been the case ever since "the bourgeois revolution of the modern period defined man's humanity by a theoretical liberty and an abstract equality, while at the same time it created a social system that effectively suppresses this equality and liberty."[17]

The principal difficulty the cultural critic faces in passing from the modern to the postmodern context is the task of defining alternate strategies that free his or her practice from the systematizing theoretical pretense that tends to make critical approaches into cover-ups for the status quo. Thus, for example, to counter the claim that politics and scholarship are to be kept separate with the claim that everything is political is neither sufficient not strategically effective. The problem, as Castoriadis points out, is that "there is no passage from ontology to politics." It is nevertheless significant that, while they are radically different in their strategy and orientation, both philosophy and politics "proceed from the same movement of putting into question the established order of society." As a result, even though a postmodern vantage has disrupted a link that seemed natural to certain kinds of modernist thought, the relation that can now be conceptualized will at least make theory less likely to fall into the self-deluded stance marking some modernist approaches: "Philosophy cannot found a politics—indeed, it cannot 'found' anything at all. In political matters in particular, all that philosophy can say is: if you want philosophy, you also must will a society in which philosophy is possible."[18] At the same time, the task of the critic is not made easier by this realization; the lack of a ground imposes the obligation of unrelenting and purposeful attention to one's words and deeds. The work of a relativist assumes implicitly a responsibility for one's own beliefs: "since the contingency of all value cannot be evaded, whoever does the *urging* cannot ultimately suppress, or ultimately evade taking responsibility for, the *particularity* of the perspective from which he does so." There is no more appealing to authority, and one of the beneficial results of relativism's application has been to ensure "that all authority was *always* subject to interrogation and *always* at risk. All authority: which must mean that of parent, teacher, and missionary as well as that of tyrant, pope, and state flunky." This includes the authority of the relativist as well; thus "the power of a justificatory theoretical account to organize and stabilize her perceptions and choices can never be altogether secure."[19]

From a postmodern vantage, however, the insecurity is a small price to pay for the lucidity that has been gained in the process. Contrary to objectivism, then, relativism "does not conceive of itself as a logical deduction, or as an inescapable conclusion drawn either from personal experience or scientific experiment, or as an insight into the underlying nature of things, or as a transcendental revelation." The relativist understands and accepts that he or she is dependent on an otherness not amenable to understanding: "This conception of the world requires that there be 'something' other than itself, other than the process of conceiving-the-world; but it cannot conceive of a single other thing to say, or way to think, about that 'something'—not a single feature to predicate of it, or any way to describe, analyze, or manipulate any of its properties— that would be *independent* of that process."[20] Furthermore, the prospect of a dependency on an unfathomable and uncontrollable otherness does not produce the urge to colonize or reject it; as David Couzens Hoy explains: "I do not know if there can be a postmodern postmodernism, but I doubt that the possibility would worry the postmodern to the degree that the possibility of the postmodern worries the modernist." This is because postmodernism "has been cured of the anxiety of influence, which is the central obsession of modernism."[21] The loss of this anxiety has also freed postmodern critique from the obligation to justify the grounds for its practice theoretically. While *ontos* and *doxa* must remain separate in a system whose principal goals are the equality and freedom of the participants, and while we await "an alternate account of our commerce with the universe *and* our commerce with each other,"[22] we can profit from the realization that the separation of these two concerns also requires their proximity. The consequences have brought about an intensification of philosophical activity and critical inquiry aiming to explain the functioning of a society cast adrift from its ideological moorings.

We have already seen that the revolutionary pretense of structuralist and poststructuralist theorizing consisted in proclaiming the end of an era and finding the proof of this in a number of exemplary deaths: those of man, humanism, and ideology. Such announcements were perhaps somewhat premature, but the claims were justified in the sense that the age was certainly witnessing a rearrangement in the conceptual configuration of its favorite motifs. The notion of "Man," understood as the norm for the essentially human, was clearly losing its credibility, and humanism has consequently been forced to undergo a fundamental revaluation; ideological discourse, likewise, was required to resituate itself in a new position of neutrality and naturalness to establish ethical legitimacy without appearing to need it. This new configuration of rationales for legitimating the socioeconomic system of Western societies has produced, in turn, theories by sociologists and political scientists that try to account for the failure of modernity on the one hand and elucidate the changes currently occurring on the other.

The countless attempts to explain our world have indeed produced "a veritable eruption of designations: postindustrial society, communication society, consumer society, society of spectacle, blocked society, bureaucratic society, monopolistic state capitalism, technocratic society, etc."[23] Romain Laufer and Catherine Paradeise, two French sociologists, propose that we see today's society in terms of an overriding strategy of marketing and an ideology they call cybernetic. In such a society, marketing has become a "bureaucratic form of sophistry." The allegorical representative of power is a Machiavellian technocrat they designate as "the bureaucratic Prince." The accession to power of this postmodern reincarnation of the Prince signals the advent of a new order of things, in which it is no longer the truth of science or reason that is the goal but the reality of appearances. In a society characterized by a cybernetic ideology, the nature of meaning is recognized as inherently contingent because "a world without a referent is devoid of sense. What is left is the infinite multiplicity of opinions. Power is nothing more than the fact of its exercise, and domination but a pragmatic question of its maintenance through the manipulation of public opinion." It is in this sense that we can understand why marketing is the contemporary, fundamentally bureaucratic form of sophistry: what counts is the pure and simple, material manifestation of opinion, not some deeper essence it might harbor or contain. The realm of essences and deeper meanings is not irrelevant—but it is a given, it is already there and continues to serve as the system of legitimation necessary for the establishment of any social order: "The efficacy of a principle of legitimacy is proportional to its capacity for defining a stable referent for social order, one situated outside society and functioning as an intangible instance of truth. This referent justifies the nature of domination and the manner in which the latter is exerted by defining the source of domination, its domains and the form of the relation between levels of power and the obeisance required of the objects of power."[24] Such an arrangement provides an eminently pragmatic solution to the problem of legitimation because simulation makes use of the already existing, well-entrenched ideology of liberalism. The ultimate referent of this cybernetic ideology is therefore a concept that is fundamental to liberal ideology—it is the idea of the individual, of individual responsibility, a concept that partakes both of a vaguely Platonic ideal of consciousness and a vulgarized, commonsensical notion of Cartesian self-sufficiency.

The purpose of liberalism was to institute a society that would respect the rights of its every member with the understanding that "all men have the same aptitude for freedom, the same original equality without distinction as to race, religion, social class. They have the right to the same security, to express their opinions . . . to engage in the activity of their choice." It is when individuals are granted these "natural" rights that they become "the countless source of social energy." In addition, in the Anglo-Saxon tradition of liberal political institutions, the individual's potential is expected to be fully realized in the context of various associations; thus "Anglo-Saxon liberalism encourages associations for profit-making, cultural, or political purposes, thus allowing for the expansion of the source of energy."[25] As a consequence, liberalism is inseparable from the economic development of capitalistic societies and has existed "in a close symbiosis with a fact still more ancient and more noteworthy, which is industrialization, material and technical progress, long-range growth."[26] Accordingly, this idealized, imaginary "liberal universe is composed of entities—of individuals—characterized by their desires. Interaction, exchange are made necessary by the quest to satisfy these desires in a universe of rarity."[27] It therefore becomes necessary to shape and manipulate this desire; furthermore, since the individual's independence is a given, the manipulation of desire is made acceptable by the assumption of freedom of choice and decision, the fundamental right that liberalism guarantees its adherents. Strategies of marketing are authorized to operate in the name of free choice and to employ the rhetoric that is necessary for convincing citizens of their desire for particular needs and products—and of their need of specific political or administrative actions. Democracy, the system that guarantees the rights of the individual, is thereby made inseparable from the free-market economic system, which is made to appear as the natural and inevitable outgrowth and complement of the former.

A cybernetic ideology consecrates the collusion between the two systems by making the existing socioeconomic arrangement appear inherently moral. As a result, discourses of morality gradually become separated from the reality they are claiming to supervise and guide: "Discourses on the virtues of Work, of Family, of Fraternity, of Equality, begin to take on more and more the appearance of pure discourses, an abuse of words replacing things, used to maintain their mythology in the face of situations that are completely heterogenous to them, and which resist, undominated, indomitable."[28] It is by founding its claim to morality in its own existence that the system becomes fundamentally amoral. Liberalism was predicated on distinctions of essence and appearance; the new ideology no longer finds the distinction useful and blends all dualities into one purely pragmatic concept: "Liberalism distinguishes between nature and culture, cybernetics merges them in the single category of the artificial; liberalism is founded on a science, cybernetic ideology constitutes itself as science. The science of liberalism separates subject from object to guarantee its objectivity, cybernetics schematizes both under the common category of system whose degree of openness depends on the goal pursued by the one using the model."[29] Thus arises the possibility of dispensing with morality and politics—the simulation of moral or political stances is deemed sufficient for ensuring the system's efficacy.

And yet it is not at all certain that the arrangement inaugurated under the auspices of a cybernetic ideology has been all that successful in its attempt to establish itself. The current controversies opposing defenders of traditional values to the critics of culture suggest that all is not well with the system. The campaign to restore morality is itself a clear indication that it is no longer possible to believe in the morality of Western civilization, on the one hand, and in the credibility of real political choices on the other: "Any clear distinctions between governmental forms and political regimes vanish to make room for pure and simple differences of managing a world economy whose decisions it is no longer possible to situate very clearly."[30] The possibility of making political choices that once held out the prospect of change and improvement in the socio-economic repartition of goods and social advantages seems to be dissipating, and the prerogatives of the haves appear more entrenched than ever. The one rationale that is still operative and helps maintain a semblance of legitimacy—or, at least, prevents a radical and massive questioning of both the accomplishments and promises of Western civilization—is the notion of prosperity. The liberal-capitalist system is still considered to be the best guarantee for individual and global prosperity and is the force that drives the incessant striving for growth, development, ever-intensifying production. But it is also becoming evident that the mechanism of unrestrained and unchecked production-consumption is kept in place by claims of civilizing, democratizing, intentions.

Consequently, the system is subject to an inescapable paradox: it cannot maintain itself without constantly renewing its legitimacy by an appeal to higher values, essences, a national destiny and a humanitarian purpose. It attempts to carry out this process of legitimation by means of a strategy of marketing techniques operating under the cover of simplistic moral tenets that it wishes to pass off as a democratic process. The system is of course forced to cover up the dichotomy of pragmatic purpose and idealistic pretense by demonstrating that such principles as freedom, equality, democracy are fundamental to its very nature and therefore justify the means it uses to sustain itself.

For the system to work, therefore, the theme of legitimacy is to be relentlessly promoted—whence the new and unrivaled importance of the sophists, who are responsible for producing the needed rhetoric, the words, the slogans that are effective, for whom "the words that work are those which, in a general manner, can resolve miraculously a problem of legitimacy (public opinion, consensus) or which eliminate a contradiction between a factual reality and a righteous aspiration (silent majority, mass culture, the heart of France)."[31] The best formulas, the most effective slogans, do not even need to be invented. They can be found by consulting public opinion, by studying what the current trends in popular thinking might be, by exploiting the fears, the hopes, and aspirations of the populace, by divining what is felt only indistinctly and then naming it forcefully, making the popular opinion discover in the newly created slogan the revelation of a truth it was struggling to discover. The formers of public opinion are, in effect, appropriating everyone's opinion, because "by means of market surveys, the Bureaucratic Prince takes the words out of the mouth of those he addresses, opening a space for a silent majority and an aphasic opposition, which will try to express itself through violence."[32] The advantage of having a silent majority is precisely its silence and passivity; the minority wishing to resist is condemned to violence and is left to discredit itself through its actions. The realm of politics thus becomes a show, a spectacle; it is the supreme art of the sophist: "If politics has become a spectacle, it is because, more than ever, it is the art of seduction, of persuasion by means of word and gesture, the art of sophistry."[33]

It is a reality that has not escaped some of the more perspicacious observers of the contemporary political scene who note that by the time public awareness began to focus on the system's viability, "government had become representative in the theatrical instead of the constitutional sense of the word. Because nobody could know what he or she was expected to know, somebody had to perform the rituals of wisdom. Somebody—the actor, the newsman, the publicist, the politician—had to pretend to be wearing a robe and crown of stars and go before the assembled cameras to say that he was the north wind. . . . In Washington what is important is the appearance of a thing and the reflection in the glass (i.e., the editorial pages of *The Washington Post*)."[34] These producers of illusions, who pretend to work to eliminate illusions by grounding thought in true values, find a fertile soil in a general commonsensical preference for the impalpable, the abstract, the transcendental. Not surprisingly, the specialists who manipulate the mirrors, who fabricate images and form opinions, are also the ones to wield political power, and it is evident that today's "sophists and marketing men seem to be in a better position with regard to the exercise of power than today's philosophers or Plato." This is because "sophistry, which is the philosophy of power, accords itself with appearances, while Plato denounces them as illusion, as a veil that must be removed to show the truth it hides."[35] The tactic elaborated by postmodern critics is the reverse: for them, truth is in the very reality of appearances—there is no need to look beyond them. Indeed, the tactic of finding truth behind appearances is that of todays sophists; and the claims of these manipulators of public opinion are becoming more and more difficult to maintain precisely because they propose as genuine those values the system clearly holds to be fiction. They are thus faced with meeting the increasingly impossible requirement of upholding a system that prevents the realization of the very values that serve to legitimize it.

The socioeconomic system of Western societies is increasingly beset by some glaring contradictions. For example, the ideological representation of the individual's rights and aspirations is contradicted by a material reality that stands in stark contrast with the representation. The ideals of freedom and equality promoted by the Enlightenment are still that—ideals to be realized. Freedom, in the experience of many, "is a privilege fully available only to those who can afford it."[36] Moreover, an individual's freedom to act and decide is inevitably limited by an environment in which individual rights and possibilities are severely constrained by corporate influence and prerogatives. It is ironic, indeed, that "in a society dedicated to the value of the individual, support of free enterprise leads to the growth of giant corporations, which foster a concern for a set of interests that increasingly undermine the importance of the individual, and hence support of free enterprise comes into conflict with the original values espoused."[37] To understand why this happened, we must see beyond "the common-sense view that persons are the fundamental elements of which a social system is composed"; we have to realize that "the rise of the modern corporation has overwhelmed the citizen in civil society and in political action."[38] Thus, the corporation, defined as a legal person, has become a member of a society that can only be termed asymmetric, since the conditions governing the relations between the two kinds of members that compose it—the corporate and the human—are more likely to be influenced by the corporate actor. A freedom thus defined in terms of a political program that holds the freedom of the marketplace as the uppermost value is most useful for making the issue of freedom impossibly confusing because it makes the interests of the individual overlap with those of the multinationals. It is in this context that the obfuscating tactics of the sophists become important. They serve the interests of the status quo by impeding thought, by diverting it to the imaginary realm of cultural values, by changing the subject literally and thus making the defense of conservative values into a radical cause. The promotion of certain values and principles must therefore be understood in light of a situation that devalues the human; therefore, the rhetoric promoting what passes for a humanistic value system needs to be reinterpreted according to its more immediate goals. The uses to which the concept of freedom is put to preserve large corporations from governmental interference is a revealing example of the subterfuge involved in the manipulation of public opinion; thus, "the emergent commercial interests invariably campaign on the promise to get the government off the backs of the people, by which they mean, of course, off the back of their own profits."[39]

The social ideals thus promoted function with a view to one overriding principle—that of performativity or efficacy. And since profit accrues most naturally to those who are in charge, the social system serves to preserve an inequality that is an inherent part of the system's strategy of self-maintenance. Inequality is, in a literal sense, institutionalized in society and is no longer attributable to differences in skill or effort but to one's particular location in the institutionally constituted hierarchy of opportunities. Just as some persons in the old social structure had the good fortune to be born into wealthy and powerful families, individuals in the current social order benefit from a strategic situation at a particular node allowing

him or her to extract proportionately greater benefits from transactions with others than is possible for those who deal from less
favorable institutional vantages. Under a system where the rights
of property take precedence over the rights of the individual, society has come to be dominated by a plutocracy that has "evolved
into a large spawn of affluent mandarins—in government, the
corporations, the professions, and the media."[40] That is why an
individual identity is turning into one of those myths that has little
relation to the practical world, and "whether lawyer, politician or
executive, the American who knows what's good for his career
seeks an institutional rather than an individual identity."[41] At the
same time, in a system that valorizes the strategic position rather
than the occupier of that position, the individual becomes "irrelevant in a fundamental sense. The person is merely an occupant of a
position in the structure and can at any time be replaced."[42] As the
sense of community dissipates, an individual's links to a particular
group are also weakened.

A postmodern critical perspective aims to disclose first the sub-
terfuges involved in the system that currently passes for being
democratic and to reveal, for example, "the cynicism of the democratic state which, however much it promises the freedom to par-
ticipate in governance, merely delivers an ersatz public sphere, an
imitation of public life."[43] Because the system is thoroughly cynical
in this regard, a useful tactic to counter its effects is to develop a
new kind of politics, a new kind of understanding befitting the
existing conditions, an approach leading to the realization that no
elements or structures exist before or outside the elaboration of
relations that put them into place: they are the products of historical
processes. Even notions of justice, of rights, develop as the result of
slow historical elaborations. A belief in transcendentals, in eternal
and universal verities, mainly serves to benefit the powers that be.
Those who hold power, for example, will benefit from maintaining the arrangement that legitimated the possession of power even
after the supporting element of this arrangement has dissipated.
Thus, the monarch's power, which used to be granted by God, has
become an empty space with the disappearance of monarchies.
This loss of foundation sheds a new light on the importance of
knowledge in determining the legitimacy of political institutions:
"Once power ceases to manifest the principle which generates and

organizes a social body, once it ceases to condense within it virtues deriving from a transcendent reason and justice, law and knowledge assert themselves as separate from and irreducible to power."[44] The lack of a ground or of metaphysical guarantees thus becomes a desirable advantage in the quest for a truly democratic society because the realm of justice and rights becomes the locus for the expression of popular will: "Democracy thus proves to be the historical society *par excellence,* a society which, in its very form, welcomes and preserves indeterminacy."[45]

It is an indeterminacy that is achieved by ridding society of all systematic determinants, of the transcendental themes of power and authority (God, ruling dynasty or class) that are used for maintaining social cohesion. Without such an overarching principle of adhesion, society becomes truly "societal" in the sense of "democratic," because "democracy is instituted and sustained by the *dissolution of the markers of certainty.* It inaugurates a history in which people experience a fundamental indeterminacy as to the basis of power, law and knowledge and as to the basis of relations between *self* and *other,* at every level of social life." Such an indeterminacy helps inaugurate a society in which the greatest participation of all the members becomes possible precisely because it is the sort of social arrangement "in which the foundations of the political order and the social order vanish, in which that which has been established never bears the seal of full legitimacy, in which differences of rank no longer go unchallenged, in which right proves to depend upon the discourse which articulates it, and in which the exercise of power depends upon conflict."[46]

On the other hand, it is also evident that in an arrangement of this nature society is always vulnerable to the danger of totalitarianism and must arm itself against the emergence of the various phantasms that feed and fulfill totalitarian urges—the notions of a unified people with a destiny, of national essence, of incarnations of power, of a deified state. The situation is never safe from the danger of subversion because the relativization of values that is a requirement for democracy can be exploited by the dominant social or professional classes. While principles underlying the founding of a society and the laws regulating the relations that determine a particular social order are perfectly manifest and subject to analysis and debate, the practice of politics frequently succeeds in occluding fundamental mechanisms that work against the principles around which a group of humans elaborates its social project. What is needed is a different conception of politics, one based on the understanding that what is "political" is not only what politicians do but what happens to the people in the social system: "The political is thus revealed, not in what we call political activity, but in the double movement whereby the mode of institution of society appears and is obscured."[47]

The reality and legitimacy of the principles on which Western societies have been instituted is in question today. To be valid, they have to be seen as something more than simple alibis. As soon as principles take on the appearance of pretexts, the entire structure they serve to support is threatened and their validity needs to be reestablished by newer and more probing discourses. It is in this dual process of questioning and legitimizing that the humanities are involved today and why they find themselves at the center of a controversy that does not always name the main points of contention.

CHAPTER 8

THE BATTLE
OVER THE HUMANITIES

Foucault, we have seen, uses the distinction provided by the French language to differentiate between two sorts of knowledge: one kind, which he designates as *savoir,* "is the process through which the subject finds [itself] modified by what [it] knows. . . . *Connaissance,* however, is the process which permits the multiplication of knowable objects, the development of their intelligibility, the understanding of their rationality, while the subject doing the investigation always remains the same."[1] What we know is only a fraction of the vast cognitive dimension informing our understanding, and while we think we are in possession of our knowledge, we are actually possessed by a *savoir* that determines not only what we can know but what we are; this truth about ourselves, moreover, is never stable because it is contingent on a dimension negated by our tendency to think only in terms of *connaissance.* Foucault therefore suggests that we begin to ask ourselves questions that will disturb our self-confident ways of knowing:

> And what if understanding the relation of the subject to the truth were just an effect of knowledge? What if understanding were a complex, multiple, non-individual formation, not "subjected to the subject," which produced effects of truth? One should then put forward positively this entire dimension which the history of science has negativised; analyse the productive capacity of knowledge as a collective practice; and consequently replace individuals and their "knowledge" in the development of a knowledge which at a given moment functions according to certain rules which one can register and describe.[2]

By making us see knowledge as the product of a collective practice, Foucault brings to our attention the highly disparate and intangible process through which reality is constituted for us. It is a reality not made up of truths but, as Betty Jean Craige puts it, of "historically grounded fictions" that are the constitutive elements of "culture's discourse—its writings, its utterances, its economic exchanges, its role definitions, its social relationships, its alliances, its wars."[3] In our culture, the humanities have had a major responsibility in the task of making sense of this disparateness, of representing and disseminating this reality. As interpreters of the cultural unconscious, they have had an important part to play in the shaping of subjects by creating models for aesthetic, ethical, and political thinking. At the same time, the humanities have been undermined by a deficiency that, as Lacan reminds us, is the signal characteristic of all human discursive activity. According to Shoshana Felman, the special significance of the unconscious in Lacan's work is attributable to "the discovery that human discourse can by definition never be entirely in agreement with itself, entirely identical to its knowledge of itself, since, as the vehicle of unconscious knowledge, it is constitutively the material locus of a signifying difference from itself."[4] But discourse can also be revealing in this regard, since it is in the gaps, the discrepancies, the ambiguities, and the faults that we discover the rules governing its functioning. Thus, at a time when the discourse on the subject of the humanities seems particularly affected by contradictory and confusing claims, such discrepancies can tell us much about the current situation of the humanities and their prospects.

To begin, we can note that the present condition of the humanities in the United States is marked by a curious paradox. On the one hand, it is apparent that, generally speaking, the reigning sociopolitical climate is hardly propitious for concerns that the practice of the humanities exemplifies. Society manifests little regard for the humanities and, although there is often talk of their importance, it would seem they are simply not considered relevant to the important economic and political concerns of the day. This reality imposes itself in myriad ways and on a daily basis, and while the evidence for the disregard in which the humanities have fallen is mostly anecdotal and scattered, it is so prevalent and so commonplace that it is difficult not to grant it the status of incontrovertible evidence; as a consequence, "within the university's hierarchy of disciplines, humanists are likely to feel more peripheral than central. Tradition gives the humanities an importance that current funding and research priorities belie. At giant public 'multiversities' like the Big Ten schools, humanities courses are taken by many students only as requirements—a sort of force-feeding in writing skills, history, great books, and appropriate 'values' before they select the chutes labeled 'preprofessional.' "[5] On the other hand, the current sociopolitical climate has also generated an unprecedented, official, governmentally sponsored campaign to revive the humanities. Not surprisingly, in light of this paradox, the campaign turns out to be a highly ambiguous undertaking, and the fierceness with which it is waged contradicts the general lack of importance the humanities have economically, politically, socially, even institutionally. The contradiction invites pondering:

> Why the humanities should have attracted so much attention and hostility when they are otherwise so universally perceived as impractical and innocuous, except in totalitarian countries, is puzzling, if not amusing. Parents who send their children to universities to major in disciplines that will help them become doctors, engineers, business managers, corporate executives, lament in chorus with seers like Secretary William Bennett and Alan Bloom and Lynne Cheney that we have lost our moral and intellectual moorings, that, of all things, we have become too "professional." We have lost our great traditions. We have been seduced by relativists into betrayal of the heritage of Plato, Dante, Shakespeare, Milton, Rousseau, and Kant (whatever that very heterogeneous heritage may have been). Literature has been made political. Standards are shattered.[6]

A central issue in the controversy surrounding the humanities is clearly the question of tradition or, more specifically, the problem of interpreting the legacy. If we consider the antecedents for such interpretations, we realize they have a long and varied history. The term itself—*humanities*—can be traced back to Roman antiquity, although the manner in which we understand it today is best related to the time of the European Renaissance: the humanities came to be known in the fifteenth century and later as the *Studia humanitas,* an area of knowledge that comprised grammar, rhetoric, poetry, history, and moral philosophy, as these terms were then understood. Subsequently, these studies developed into a large body of philosophical, historical, and literary knowledge; as the 1980 "Report of the Commission on the Humanities" explains, "For centuries the fields of knowledge most often viewed as humanistic have been languages and literatures, history, and philosophy." But, it goes on to point out, "to these the Commission on the Humanities of 1963–64 added the arts, 'the history and comparison of religion and law,' and 'those aspects of the social sciences which have humanistic content and employ humanistic methods.' Legislation authorizing the National Endowment for the Humanities— the Report adds—now also includes linguistics, archaeology, and ethics."[7] Furthermore, in *Webster's Third New International Dictionary,* the "humanities" are defined as "the branches of learning regarded as having primarily a cultural character and usu. including languages, literature, history, mathematics, and philosophy." It seems clear, then, that the cognitive area encompassed by the notion of the humanities is quite broad and still likely to expand. It is equally clear that the fields of knowledge constituting the humanities do not alone define the essence of the humanities and that we have to look for some other way of specifying the particular nature of the human activity and concerns over which this term lays claim.

Such definitions are not hard to come by. The 1980 Commission on the Humanities provides us with a fairly typical one. According to the commission, "the essence of the humanities is a spirit or an attitude toward humanity. They show how the individual is autonomous and at the same time bound, in the ligatures of language and history, to humankind across time and throughout the world."[8] The problem with such definitions is that while at first they may sound quite valid and appear to express some unimpeachable truth, upon closer examination they seem so vague as to become inapplicable to concrete situations. As a result, it becomes quite apparent that they have been devised mainly to serve a decorative purpose and that everyday, down-to-earth reality is both more modest and more intractable. Rather than persuade, they tend to direct our attention to the discrepancy between rhetoric and reality, between the claims made for the humanities and the concrete and verifiable benefits to be garnered. And indeed, if we wish to consider the debate surrounding the existence, the role, and the significance of the humanities today, the one theme that recurs with the greatest insistence is the sometimes obvious, sometimes implied divergence between the claims and their credibility. It is this gap, or lack, that would seem to constitute an essential aspect of the humanities today.

To be sure, the existence of the gap is no longer a secret, and its acknowledgment can be taken as evidence for the currently perceived crisis in the humanities. To cite but one example: Frank Rhodes, the president of Cornell University, has noted that "there is an alarming gap between the pretensions of the liberal arts and their performance, between the profession of those who teach the liberal arts and their contribution."[9] Such an assertion reflects the currently growing suspicion that the humanities promise much but deliver little. Opposed to this perception we have the more traditional and uncritical view we saw expressed by the 1980 Commission on the Humanities, one based on "the premise that the humanities are widely undervalued and often poorly understood."[10]

Although the two views differ in regard to their critical perspective—Rhodes places his outside the humanities, the commission speaks from within—they both bring up the same fundamental issue: that of the purpose of the humanities. It is on this question that current rationales are at their most divergent. The arguments promoting the humanities today generally take two separate tacks. One seeks to legitimate them by referring them to some golden age of humanistic values that needs only to be rediscovered to be revived. According to this particular viewpoint, the humanities have everything to do with an essence of humanity, with moral and civic virtues, which are all to be recovered in the written record of great and noble thought. Over the last few years, the best-known proponent of this approach has been William Bennett, the secretary of education in the Reagan administration. The former secretary holds firmly to the view that "intellectual refinement and spiritual elevation are the traditional goals of the humanities and should remain so."[11]

In contrast with this traditional rationale, we have a basically pragmatic argument that formulates the issues in terms of one single overriding concern—that for the marketplace and its effects. This argument promotes an unabashed selling of the humanities: to our students and their parents, to our colleagues in other disciplines, to businessmen and politicians. Some of the arguments have become familiar by now: liberal arts graduates are more flexible, broad-minded, and adaptable than students educated in more narrow fields of specialization; they are very trainable, they are better communicators, are more effective at dealing with people and tend to advance more rapidly up the corporate ladder.

There are a number of success stories to back up these claims. For example, we are told that, of the thirteen top executives at IBM, nine have liberal arts degrees—including the chairman of the board, who has a B.S. in political science. Liberal arts majors also made up a majority in Reagan's cabinet. Lynne Cheney has justified the usefulness of a liberal arts degree by citing a study made by AT&T, which "showed social-science and humanities graduates moving into middle management faster than engineers and doing at least as well as their business and engineering counterparts in reaching top management levels."[12] The recently issued report by the Ohio Board of Regents entitled *Towards the Year 2000* notes that "college and university placement officers report a significant increase in the number of companies recruiting liberal arts students because of their abilities to think critically and creatively; write and speak well; understand and get along with co-workers; and show greater openness to change."[13]

One of the principal exponents of the practical rationale promoting the humanities again happens to be Bennett, for whom the humanities represent a most effective way of combining the virtues of learning with its practical applications. He once explained to a group of business leaders the advantages of having our students read great works of literature: "If we want our students to learn the high costs of rashness and the value of sticking to strategy," he told the group, "we should have them read Plutarch's account of the Roman consul Fabius. . . . Do we want our future business leaders to learn the dangers of an overly active ambition? Have them read *Macbeth* . . . do we want our children to know the pitfalls of playing on the job? Teach them *Anthony and Cleopatra*."[14]

Bennett's promotion of both the elitist and the practical strategies could of course be deemed curious. But perhaps this is not as great a paradox as it might first appear. From the perspective of a worldview that holds the notion of the marketplace as the overriding philosophical principle, the enjoyment of a socially superior status can be justified as the result of a process of natural selection;

thus the prerogative of the chosen few is sanctioned by the merit of the individual who rises above the ordinary many through force of character and personal effort. That the intellectual polish acquired from the study of noble thought should also serve to advance one's career is a circumstance that fits quite nicely into the socioeconomic scheme and can therefore be viewed as a welcome and deserved advantage for those favored by the system. The humanities are thus helped to regain the importance they had in the nineteenth century, when they provided a cultural identity for upwardly mobile sons of the bourgeoisie.

The humanities, as we know them, are indeed a product of the nineteenth century. Specifically, they evolved in an institutional setting that was modeled after the German university. The German system had been devised by Wilhelm von Humboldt, according to whom higher education was to make the pursuit of truth coincide with the pursuit of just ends in moral and political life; it was to provide the young men who were to form the ruling sociopolitical elite with the necessary *Bildung*—a concept denoting both formation of mind and character and describing a process that provides education cum cultural polish. According to this scheme, "Research and the spread of learning are not justified by invoking a principle of usefulness"; on the contrary, "knowledge finds legitimacy within itself" and its value is determined by the place it occupies "in the itinerary of Spirit or Life."[15] It seems clear, then, that in recent years this last Hegelian theme has been gradually replaced by the principle of usefulness, and it would appear that the principle of *l'honnête homme*—the classical French notion of what constituted cultural polish—has been replaced by that of *homo oeconomicus*.[16]

Of course, the official versions purporting to explain the situation of the humanities tell a completely different story. Lynne Cheney, in her "Report to the President, the Congress, and the American People" entitled *Humanities in America,* notes that at a time when "people outside the academy are increasingly turning to literary, historical, and philosophical study, are increasingly finding the 'good arts' a source of enrichment for themselves and their society," the study of the humanities in our colleges and universities has declined, the humanities themselves are in disarray, professors feel demoralized and isolated and are haunted by "a lost sense of meaning in academic humanities." To illustrate her claim that society is undergoing a dramatic humanistic rebirth, Cheney cites statistics pointing to the rising number of participants in events organized by humanities councils, the increased attendance in museums, the participation in library reading programs and the fact that while "in 1970 total spending for admission to cultural events was less than half that for sports events in the United States . . . in 1986 the total spending to attend cultural events *exceeded* the amount spent on spectator sports by 10 per cent." The numbers she uses to illustrate the neglect of the humanities in our nation's colleges and universities, while familiar to many of us, are equally dramatic. Thus, "in 1988–89, it is possible to earn a bachelor's degree from: 37 per cent of the nation's colleges and universities without taking *any* course in history; 45 per cent without taking a course in American or English literature; 62 per cent without taking a course in philosophy; 77 per cent without studying a foreign language."[17] Cheney lays the blame squarely at the door of the professors and administrators of our institutions of higher learning. Her reasons for doing so are various and echo the concerns frequently voiced by William Bennett: professors are more interested in their research than in teaching, their research is often esoteric, too theoretical and too specialized to be of any value to the student; there are those who tend to politicize the study of the humanities and to give greater weight to feminist and ethnic studies than the Western tradition.

For Cheney, there exist two opposing camps: the universities on one side and society on the other—each camp representing an autonomous and unified entity. What opposes them is a truly ironic contrast: while the humanities flourish in society, they are neglected in academe. Moreover, according to Cheney, the universities have only themselves to blame; that is, they cannot have recourse to the traditional liberal argument which holds socioeconomic conditions responsible for various social ills. While ordinary people are learning to love good books and cultural events, universities allow their professors to indulge in irrelevant research and to entertain paranoid fantasies about the political significance of texts.

What is clearly missing in Cheney's analysis is any consideration of the particular circumstances and forces that make the university what it is today. In light of radically changed social expectations and cultural pressures, much of the traditional rhetoric concerning the educational and cultural role of institutions of higher education suffers from an irrelevance that is becoming more obvious every day. First to be considered is the whole issue of knowledge and its value in today's society. While it is true that "most Americans now earn their living by working with knowledge—transmitting it, transforming it, applying it, deriving it, selling it," and while in this regard colleges and universities strive to prepare students for the so-called real world, the emphasis is placed on the professional competency and expertise to be claimed, not on the enrichment of one's soul. In this, the colleges are perfectly responsible and responsive to the demands of society and, if we consider the history of higher education not from the perspective of the myths in which universities themselves are wont to indulge but from that of the needs they are expected to serve, we have to conclude, with the scholars who have studied the question, that "by and large the American university came into existence to serve and promote professional authority in society."[18] This is to suggest that, to a considerable degree, it is the culture of professionalism that sets the priorities and establishes the values to live by in our society. The rewards promised by higher education are a factor of the cultural and economic forces that have already shaped the outlook of many students before they come to the university. Thus, professors are forced to confront the fact that students, with a few welcome exceptions, "have not come to college to understand the nature of the universe or even to master a discipline or deepen their knowledge of one of its areas. They have come for grades."[19] Students seem to know instinctively that their education has no intrinsic value, that it is useless in and of itself; they know its value resides in its marketability and that the diploma is not desirable because it makes one useful to one's society or to humanity but because it promises to place its holder in an advantageous position in the arena of economic opportunity. Jerry Herron states very bluntly that "the university no longer works; it no longer represents the culture that it nominally serves and is supported by." The university is no longer needed to transmit culture that is no more than an "exhausted fetish": it is concerned with the world of work.[20]

The university is therefore intimately involved with society, and its functioning is dictated by economic and political considerations—not by a concern to impart the love of knowledge. There is little left of the traditional notion of the ivory tower, an idea promoted at the beginning of the century by Cardinal Newman: "In the course of a hundred years Cardinal Newman's university has become a nostalgic fiction, for technology has rendered illusory any separation of the academy from the capitalist culture supporting it."[21] That is why rationales claiming to preserve the university's apolitical status appear either particularly obtuse or ingenuous. Some of today's loudest critics of higher education are conservatives who speak in the name of timeless reason and who blame their opponents for politicizing the universities. Their own stance is assumed to be apolitical because, as Jay Parini has pointed out, "politics, for conservatives, can only mean left-wing politics—the leveling instincts of 'radicals' who would open the faculty club to women, blacks, and other minority professors who would trash Milton and Homer in favor of Toni Morrison or, worse, some unheard of poet from Namibia or Guadalupe."[22] The thinking of the conservative critics thus illustrates the truth of a well-known hermeneutical principle, "the axiom that in any social order, attempts to challenge the *status quo* are likely to be perceived as biased, while uncritical support of it tends to be regarded as neutral."[23]

The debate about the politicization of the curriculum is therefore based on a highly dubious premise. The interesting political issue is elsewhere: it concerns the demand that the humanities imbue students with a civic and moral outlook that has clearly depreciated within the larger sociocultural context. The question that occurs to more and more members of the teaching profession is why has it suddenly become so urgent to inspire this love of philosophy and literature in an unwilling and uninspired constituency? At a time when Madison Avenue and Hollywood seem to set the principal guidelines for social behavior, why are the humanities asked to play a role once carried out by the church? Why should professors suddenly be expected to counteract the apathy and vocational orientation of their students? Why are teachers in elementary and secondary schools similarly being held responsible for inculcating values the parents of the students often consider irrelevant? What are the reasons behind the current obsession with "reclaiming a legacy"? Are the humanities being revived to help celebrate the high achievements of our culture at a time when these have become dubious? Are they to divert our attention away from the fundamental failures of our civilization, from the growing inequities in our society, the racism and crass materialism of our social ethos? Are they perhaps expected to give dignity to a culture whose hallmarks have become Disneyland and "Terminator" movies? Idle questions? Perhaps. Yet the fact that they come up today clearly indicates that something has happened to radically alter the relationship between institutions of education and society at large; it is something that may well be motivating the attacks against universities and the demands placed on the educational system.

As I have suggested earlier, Foucault's distinction between two fundamental ways of knowing and of producing knowledge is helpful for sorting out and clarifying some of the issues concerning the uses and the history of the humanities. We can note, first, that in one respect the distinction between a radical and a conservative stance is moot. In light of Foucault's understanding, all who are involved with the teaching of the humanities are engaged in a fundamentally conservative practice. Feminists, Marxists, as well as members of the National Association of Scholars, are all involved in a project whose purpose is to control the process of knowledge, to transmit and to develop forms of *connaissance,* and once this is accomplished, to help maintain the knowing subject in a relatively stable condition: the syllabi we produce, the departmental and college curricula, no matter how radical and innovative their claims, are all institutional ways of ensuring some continuity and permanence.

That, at least, is the pretense behind which we operate; but schemes for ensuring continuity and permanence can never be more than a pretense because knowledge is never strictly a *connaissance:* it is always already a *savoir.* Therefore any attempt at controlling processes of cognition is undermined from the start by the irreducible symbolic dimension that gives rise to a *savoir* in a society, a dimension that does not lend itself to surveys, anthologizing, or analyses and that mocks our desire to claim mastery over it. Knowledge presenting itself as a self-sufficient domain of cognition does so by ignoring the ineffable in culture, by denying its links with the formative matrix of the cultural unconscious that has given it its shape—it has to ignore its own ignorance. One of the notable merits of psychoanalytical theory has been to disclose the extent to which ignorance is "no longer simply *opposed* to knowledge: it is itself a radical condition, an integral part of the very *structure* of knowledge." As a consequence, the knowledge that we propose to process, to advance, and to disseminate is only "a kind of *unmeant knowledge* which escapes intentionality and meaning, a knowledge which is spoken by the language of the subject (spoken, for instance, by his 'slips' or by his dreams), but which the subject cannot recognize, assume as *his,* appropriate; a speaking knowledge which is nonetheless denied to the speaker's knowledge."[24] Thus any attempt to impose knowledge with a view toward preserving the stability of the knowing subject turns out to be an exercise in futility. At the same time we have to recognize that some exercises are more futile than others.

In this regard, one of the more futile is certainly the project to establish canons for wisdom, to canonize sources of knowledge. It is an endeavor that is moved by a belief in an immutable and absolute subject of knowledge—an entity whose identity is given once and for all. Such an attempt is clearly driven by notions of *telos,* origin, and essence that are the integral components of philosophies promoting what could be termed a "metaphysical eschatology." It is a mode of thought that is both mystified and mystifying because it "tells the story of a privileged and primordial *ethos* and the great beginning, prior to the subject–object split, and it looks ahead to a new dawn, which is to be an eschatological repetition and renewal of what began in the first dawn, before metaphysics and all metaphysical ethics."[25]

The discourse of origins, ends, and essences is an integral part of the philosophy of humanism that still serves to cover up the lack of discernible connections between thought and history, great books and morality. It is a discourse that also hides the political effects of a strategy of defending "the canon": by maintaining education in the mode of a *connaissance,* the identity of the subject is preserved; the humanities thus become an essential part of the process determining the subject; they help create an identity for individuals that fits into the existing pattern of social norms and hierarchies—that corresponds to the basic andro- and ethnocentricity of culture, for example. In this manner, the humanities become a true discipline in the Foucaultian sense; they become an integral part of a disciplinary power whose main purpose is to make "of a person an individual with properties which can be scrutinized and categorized into bodies of theoretical knowledge. That is, the individual is sundered from any relations which would concretize who he or she is. In the place of such a person, an atomic individual emerges whose only distinguishing features are properties shared by any other individual."[26] Consequently, those who would have us subscribe to an immutable canon are really calling for the imposition of a *connaissance* that passes as *savoir,* an artificial *savoir* that works as a systematized program for ensuring ignorance about the actual processes determining the subject.

Foucault, we have seen, wishes to provide an understanding that will help individuals remove themselves from the abstract conceptual network that facilitates the application of power. By freeing themselves from abstract norms, individuals are able to establish identities in terms of the concrete experiences that relations with others provide. At the same time we have to understand that freedom is not to be interpreted as offering the possibility to sever all ties. Freedom "is only possible within the terms of membership in a society; these terms, however, are not foundational but are produced by society itself."[27] Foucault discounted explanations that propose stable determinisms for creating identity; thus, he found the notion of ideology and ideological struggle unsatisfactory because, as he put it, "the theoretical coordinates of each of us are often, no, always, confused and fluctuating, especially if they are observed in their genesis."[28] The experience of writing was a way for him of testing these theoretical coordinates and of providing, for himself, as well as for his readers, an opportunity to modify them: "I invite others to share the experience. That is, an experience of our modernity that might permit us to emerge from it transformed."[29] Instead of attempting to control knowledge, a Foucaultian approach invites its practitioners to investigate the configuration and genealogy of different kinds of knowledges, to identify and explore the links these knowledges establish with one another as well as with other, unofficial, and sometimes hidden knowledges. Such an approach produces, as well, a new understanding of teaching—one that more adequately addresses the nature of *savoir:* "Teaching thus, is not the transmission of ready-made knowledge, it is rather the creation of a new *condition* of knowledge—the creation of an original learning disposition."[30]

Foucault sought to create new conditions for knowledge by working out what he called an ontology of the present. He showed that the elaboration of such an ontology requires that we neither reject nor scorn the past but that we accept it as an integral part of what makes us the subjects we are. On the other hand, neither is the past to be exalted at the expense of the factors determining our position as subjects in the current sociopolitical and cultural discursive and institutional arrangement. Viewed in this perspective, the humanities are to be seen not so much as an instrument for accomplishing ethical or aesthetic ideals, for realizing a nature or accomplishing a destiny, but as the best source of information about what is happening around us and—therefore—within us. Likewise, postmodern theories do not pretend to influence or to transcend the current sociohistorical juncture, knowing full well that "any transcendence will only be the accomplishment of social practices themselves." To blame the poststructuralists or anyone else for the current disarray in the humanities is to rely on an antiquated explanatory model of thought: "Derrida did not invent the decentering of the self, the self is already in the process of being decentered. Derrida, Levinas, Heidegger, and others are only chroniclers; their power rests only in a capacity to focus public attention. Philosophy follows history."[31]

While the poststructuralists have chronicled and postmodernists continue to document the disintegration of modernity, they have also made us anticipate the emergence of a new understanding. H. G. Wells was able to observe some sixty years ago already that "human history becomes more and more a race between education and catastrophe." The truth of this observation is if anything even more relevant to our situation today. The most important role that the humanities can therefore have is that of helping us understand what we are, how we got here, and how best to proceed from here. Today it is safe to say that the humanities do not simply concern the great works of philosophy and literature of the past but encompass much that is outside and goes counter to the traditionally circumscribed realms of literary and philosophic studies; their purpose is not to help realize universal structures of knowledge but to articulate what we think and what we are at a given moment in history.

Consequently, we can no longer limit ourselves to Western or Eurocentric modes of expression but need to acknowledge a changing reality by seeing that the humanities are being redefined by thinkers and writers who are no longer exclusively Western, white, and male. We are thus witnessing the waning of a model of the humanities that owed its legitimacy to notions of cultural, national, race and gender-oriented superiority and we are seeing such prejudices quite appropriately being relegated to the storehouse of cultural relics. Doubtless, such a state of affairs has already caused and will continue to produce anguish and insecurity. These impressions are the inevitable consequences of a cultural upheaval, but they are also the signs of a time when the most auspicious kind of thinking will inevitably challenge and tend to undermine the established norms and monuments. It is the kind of thinking that will open up different perspectives and help inaugurate a new age in which the humanities will continue to serve their vital purpose in our never-ending quest for an understanding of what makes us human.

CONCLUSION

T HE POSTURE OF the intellectual claiming a serene and rational control over the realm of his cogitation has turned out to be an imposture. The methods that made it possible to preserve a separation between intellect and the world in order to enact the former's salutary agency over the latter are no longer available. Gone is the possibility of relying on the purposeful autonomy offered by the *Cogito;* what stands out today is Descartes's naïveté, which is "to have believed that he could 'think' without language, that he could 'rid himself' of language in favor of reason, at the very moment he was obeying the unsurpassable constraints of language, at the very moment he was interpreting things according to a schema inherent to language—a schema belonging not to a pure mind but indispensable to a living man determined to appropriate the world and affirm his power."[1] The subterfuge involved in this procedure of self-legitimation has gradually come to light as a discrepancy between promises and accomplishments, between hopeful allegations and the evidence of experience. The exclusions and occlusions enacted by the assertion of a self-sufficient, autonomous source of truth identified as reason are now the subjects deemed important. Thus, in the humanities "it has become apparent within many disciplines that more attention needs to be paid to those who have been more the victims than the beneficiaries of splendors of Western culture: workers, women, blacks, Jews, colonial peoples, Native Americans, and other minorities."[2] These elisions, made possible by the application of standards deemed universal, have been magnified by the recent attempts to restore traditional paradigms of thought. While the arguments promoting a return to a culture of correct values undeniably carry a strong emotional appeal, they display an inconsistency that is symptomatic of the entire system's vulnerability. Consequently, they tend to self-deconstruct, since the axiological system they aim to revive displays "an ever increasing difficulty with generating, and making plausible, a legitimation capable of presenting the working of the system as something else than a quasi-natural and uncontrolled process."[3]

In this country the notion that sums up the process is the marketplace, a ubiquitous concept used both as an explanation and a justification for the existing cultural, socioeconomic, and political arrangement. The marketplace also epitomizes the principal difficulty afflicting the system, which is its inability to base its claims of legitimacy on anything but its own idealized and nebulous representation of itself. Because the marketplace is, by definition, amoral, the alleged morality of the system is derived not from some profound or eternal truth but from a practical need to appear moral, since a "free market" society is constrained "by the force of common law and the respect for rules of 'proper behavior,' by the maintenance of a tradition rife with rituals, moral values, beliefs, whose truth matters little so long as they are obeyed." The truth of these beliefs thus becomes amenable to manipulation and is subsumed, in effect, to the needs of the marketplace; as a result, the necessity to impose an ethical code "is accompanied by a kind of immorality: since the concept of society determines neither particular goals nor order, shows little concern for social justice but demands a clever manipulation of symbolic efficacy."[4] In this light, the current battle over the humanities could well be inscribed within a general struggle to co-opt the symbolic efficacy of cultural discourse in order to keep it from serving needs other than those of the marketplace—that is, of the established socioeconomic and political interests. The attempt to preserve the apolitical stance of academic institutions can therefore be ascribed to the ever more pressing need to provide the current sociopolitical order with a cultural, humanistic, morally legitimating facade.

The strategies defending the system are also becoming transparent, because they cannot help but enunciate and reveal the vested interests that are at stake in the debate.[5] In addition, they point to the principal subject of their concerns, which is a fear of losing the power, prestige, and privileges that once were associated with the control of a particular cultural domain: "The notion that study of the humanities used to represent, be based on, transmit, intellectual (and perhaps moral) authority reminds us that the humanities were traditionally held to represent the place of values in education. Teachers of literature, in particular, were supposed to be the guardians of a secular scripture which, in a postsacred society, contained the spiritual truths needed even by those who were to go on to be physicians, lawyers and engineers."[6] To cover up this very pragmatic and, one might say, undignified purpose motivating the promotion of the humanities,

> there is a great show of making the cultural tradition available to the people through education and the extremely generous support of public cultural institutions; and stress is placed on achieving continuity in history and civilization, on harvesting for modern life the finest of the human patrimony. The purpose, however, is to stabilize the structures of authority, to freeze the intellectual status quo while channeling initiative into material progress—that is, into economic, industrial, and, to some degree, military programs—to discipline mental and moral energies.[7]

Or, to put it very simply and very plainly, for the defenders of the status quo, "in the cultural domain, the strategy calls for reestablishment of 'traditional' values that link religion and patriarchy to the free market."[8] It is a strategy that has worked effectively until now because its politics were unmentionable and thus kept hidden.

The bringing to light of this heretofore occluded dimension has been branded a severe breach of scholarly etiquette and labeled an unwarranted politicization of the academy. The ingenuousness of these accusations is fairly transparent: the danger a politicization of academic discourse poses is especially great for the defenders of the canon because the moral advantage of their position is a prerogative to be enjoyed on condition the position's political pedigree remain occluded. The fear of losing the power derived from a maintenance of the status quo in academe has produced an agenda of law and order; that is why, in the current debates around the practice of the humanities, "there is a more or less articulated subtext implying that the restoration of the humanities and the institution of core curricula are to be devices of social control."[9] To hide this concern, the traditionalist discourse is forced to underwrite a separation between the political and the cultural that appears increasingly quixotic. While the revival of the traditional values and canon is deemed to offer new hope and solutions for problems besetting humankind, "the current rhetoric about the humanities does not seem to have much to say about the troubling social context in which these goods are to be achieved."[10] But this lapsus is also quite understandable because it is part of a political strategy at the service of an ideology of individual incentive and moral responsibility. Such an ideology offers the defenders of the system a moral stance that gives them two important advantages: it preserves them from assuming responsibility for the hopelessness and social pathology the system generates and it gives them the possibility of criminalizing the products of this pathology and hopelessness. It is therefore opportune to view the latest attempts to innovate in the humanities as betrayals of intellectual integrity, as a perversion of the lofty goals of truth and objectivity because "such intense criticism of the humanities provides a very convenient and pious-sounding diversion from the serious social problems that have much more to do with our present difficulties than the failure of students to read Plato, professors' devotion to deconstruction or even Marxism, or the humanities' failure to inculcate a concern for Western morality."[11]

The ingenuousness and incoherence frequently displayed by the arguments of those who would clean up the humanities also point to the inadequacy of the old rhetoric, to the ineptitude traditional rationales reveal when confronting the power of new ideas:

> Unease about this kind of power is reflected in a blatant contradiction that one finds repeatedly in Bennett, Cheney and Kimball: on the one hand, the allegation that the new forms of humanistic study have alienated students, purported to have deserted humanities courses in droves, and on the other hand the assertion that the radicals have laid hold of the minds of the vast majority of the young, and are indoctrinating them in their perverse ideologies. The contradiction is on a par with their critique of "overspecialization" in humanistic scholarship, matched to their complaint that the interdisciplinary ambitions of this scholarship have subverted the specific definition of literature.[12]

Furthermore, the fear reactionaries have of losing their influence is attributable to an exaggerated notion of intellectual efficacy that is very much a part of a paranoia fed by modernity. Consequently, the critics of the new ideas are wont to overrate both the subversive potency of the innovators as well as the potential of their own reforms for arresting the course of events or even turning back the clock. The speciousness of such a view is illustrated by a simple yet incontrovertible fact: "The temptation of restoring the best in our tradition of Western civilization is seductive, but . . . had we abided by the best in our tradition we would have a different one and wouldn't be where we are—which incidentally is where tradition has lost its credibility."[13] The urge to restore Western humanism to its former glory therefore suffers from a presumptuousness that appears particularly fatuous in light of the failure of whatever may have been "the best in our tradition." The proponents of reform implicitly assume the wisdom of an understanding they legitimately cannot allege: from a postmodern perspective, any claim to transform the world constitutes a subterfuge because "to conceive the world as transformable is already to have interpreted it. No one would have had either the idea or the wish to transform the world if one had not already started by understanding it. Understanding, interpretation and practice or practical application are the three moments of the same procedural unity."[14] Projects for civilizing the world are usurpations of wisdom. They are power plays that can only proceed by covering up the lack of any comprehensive and cogent understanding of what is at stake.

This distrust of the civilizing and universalizing claim of Western reason has produced a counterdiscourse that aims to uncover what has typically remained unsaid, unspecified, even unidentified but has operated anonymously under the cover of reason's guarantee of progress. This counterdiscourse also recognizes that "metaphysical 'truths' simply express the subjective values of a given individual or social group, not the immutable, unchanging essence of either the divine, human or natural world."[15] It thus strives to identify the real subject of a discourse, which is not the grammatical subject but whatever is speaking through the latter. Such a procedure has led critics to discover the organization of interests operating beneath the protective cover of an officially proclaimed superiority of Western civilization. It has come to recognize that beneath its civilizing claims, "Western modernity is driven to conquer, it presents itself as exclusive . . . it aims to create a world unified by increasingly identical needs (governed by merchandise and the market), or by a unique and expansive ideological allegiance exploiting totalitarian potentialities."[16] Thus theory is led to confront the reality elided by an urge to rationalize, to make society transparent to the rational, scientific mind. In light of the chaotic reality that is adumbrated by the theoretical investigations of poststructuralist and postmodern critics, it is the project to make the world rational that now appears questionable:

> Whatever the power of rationality, and precisely as *a direct consequence* of its power, lucid thinking (also rational) can and must proclaim that the *integral* rationalization of life is the most demented project in History. Inverting the sign of all the beneficial contributions of rationalism, this kind of rationalization brings about the ruin of all it wanted to save. From positive, it turns suicidal. Everyone will be able to find in contemporary history, unfortunately without difficulty, new examples of projects of pacification that degenerate in genocide, of missions of development that ensue in ethnocide, etc.[17]

It would appear then that the undertaking initiated by Descartes—the project of elaborating a discourse of reason as an instrument for establishing perfect control over the real and for guaranteeing progress in human affairs—has in effect produced the opposite of what it sought: the attempt to rationalize, to reduce everything to technique, to standards of efficiency and productivity, has exposed the forces of the uncontrollable, the unknowable, and the unpredictable. The dissolution of the metaphysical subject has uncovered an intimidating and bewildering complexity of forces, motives, reasons, effects, and impulses. In short, we have discovered the chaos that reigns under the occlusive hegemony of the Cartesian subject. Conscious thought is no longer seen as determining but as dependent on a dimension for which the official, culturally validated subject serves as cover. Feminist critique has helped to tear down the pretense by disclosing the patriarchal ideology at the heart of traditional humanism. At the center of this ideology, as Toril Moi describes it, "is the seamlessly unified self—either individual or collective—which is called 'Man.' . . . In this humanist ideology the self is the *sole author* of history and of the literary text: the humanist creator is potent, phallic and male—God in relation to his world, the author in relation to his text. History or the text become nothing but the 'expression' of this unique individual."[18]

The claims of universal and objective themes are gradually losing their power to occlude their androcentric orientation. Similarly, grand narratives centered on notions of national, ethnic, historical, or religious preeminence appear increasingly idiosyncratic. The impoverished rationales that still serve to lend a universal justification to historically circumscribed modes of social and cultural existence have given rise, as their counterparts, to ever more prevalent effects of indeterminism and insecurity:

> In the technocratic age, reducing the complexity of life to the single dimension of productive efficiency and material well-being has brought about the paradoxical result of a kind of uncontrollable explosion of indeterminism, both in forms of knowledge and of individual and social life. The absence of absolute foundations for knowledge and morality that characterizes our time, the fragmentation of knowledge due to the emphasis on specialization, the infinite aspect of productive activity, the questioning of traditional principles of rationality and of the very reality of the subject, the discovery of the unconscious—are all elements that have contributed to the fact that today the dimension of indeterminacy has burst forth at the very core of the determinate: in the production of material goods, in science, nature, rationality.[19]

The revelation of this indeterminacy is the principal threat to traditional ideas. It also accounts for the power and attraction exerted by the new ideas, not because they promise change but because they help fashion a new awareness and a new understanding. The work of interpretation is therefore at the center of postmodernist concerns. They posit it as an endless task, taking our apprehension of the world to be subject to a fundamental and inescapable indeterminism, to a profound *méconnaissance*. Paradoxically, this insufficiency of human reason is not construed as a shortcoming but as a distinct advantage postmodernist approaches have over modernist ones. A postmodern approach has the advantage of accepting and recognizing that human relations and perceptions are mediated by an irreducible otherness which is not amenable to appropriation or rational control. This is why the Nietzschean approach, summed up in the notion of "a philosophy of morning," is anything but nihilistic in the ordinary sense of the term:

> "A philosophy of morning" is precisely the kind of thought that is oriented towards proximity rather than towards the origin or foundation. This way of thinking about proximity could also be defined as a way of thinking about error, or better still, about erring. . . .

Given that there is no longer a truth or a *Grund* that could contradict or falsify the tissue of erring, all these errors are to be understood as kinds of roaming or wandering; for they embody the process of becoming of spiritual formations whose only rule is a certain historical continuity that is in turn devoid of any relationship to a fundamental truth.[20]

Indeed, it is when it recognizes the lack of an a priori morality or rationality that the intellect can best contribute to establishing a credible system of values. Such a procedure is especially salutary when it comes to creating and putting democratic values into effect because a democratic society is not preordained but always in process; it represents a never-ending succession of compromises, pacts, and agreements that are in need of endless renegotiation; "democracy thus reveals itself to be the historical society *par excellence,* a society, which, in its form welcomes and preserves indeterminism."[21] Calls for a new "moral rearmament" that do not provide for ways to enhance the deployment of collective initiatives and judgment are simply attempts at bypassing democratic processes.

Indeterminacy thus becomes the principal subject of postmodern critique, in the sense that it is what is allowed, encouraged to speak through it. While the notion of the subject reveals the determining strictures and influences constituting its reality, it can also become a vehicle for procedures allowing it to escape these strictures: "The subject is never simply the determination of its social identity, but also the indeterminate, the capacity for recognizing the limits of determinisms and thus to escape the intersubjective structure of the social, a structure seen as a predetermined system of relations."[22] The new theoretical approaches have sought to institute a reversal in all our familiar ways of thinking, allowing us to break out of set patterns of thought and to investigate the otherness that a strict adherence to criteria of objectivity and rationality has excluded from consideration. The radical forms of criticism that characterize the more innovative aspects of the humanities today are therefore part of a project that "must be fully implicated in the much more radical pursuit of the unknown rather than the always-already-known-but-merely-forgotten; and it must be fully implicated in the ethics of alterity. Otherwise, one remains entirely within the totalizing and dominating powers of theory, and fails to reach the emancipatory and radical potential of the postmodern moment 'after theory.' "[23] The aims of intellectuals, of the practitioners of the humanities, are modified accordingly, in order to "separate intelligence from the paranoia that made 'modernity.' "[24] For the critic this becomes a project of making the subject undergo a transformation that amounts to a demotion, to a diminution of its claims and pretenses.[25] Thus, for Vattimo, the crisis of humanism "is most likely to be resolved in terms of a kind of 'crash diet for the subject,' one which would allow the subject to listen to the call of a Being that no longer arises in the peremptory tone of the *Grund* or the thought of thought (or absolute spirit), but that dissolves its presence-absence into the network offered by a society increasingly transformed into an extremely sensitive organism of communication."[26]

The results of intellectual or critical activism, or rather, the promise of results, are likely to be less dramatic; yet it may be preferable for reasons Foucault once gave, saying "I prefer even these partial transformations that have been made in the correlation of historical analysis and the practical attitude,.to the programs for the new man that the worst political systems have repeated through the twentieth century."[27] In this perspective, the anguish identified by Roland Barthes turns out to be little more than a vestige of a rather romantic ethos according to which the intellectual's lot is a heroically tragic destiny that leaves him forever "thirsting for and wounded by a responsibility" that since the time of Rousseau he is neither able to "completely honor or completely evade."[28] The ethos was mainly a pose—a self-consciously tragic stance imbued with a sense of self-veneration.

There is also no great need to feel anguished about the fate of the humanities today. Far from posing a threat to the humanities, the new theories have obviously reinvigorated them, giving humanistic studies a new significance and urgency. To many, it seems undeniable that "the humanities, and particularly, the departments of literature, are where the action is in the American academy. These are the only places where something is happening which gets widely discussed among the professors, intrigues some of the best students, and upsets the administrators."[29] And has upset quite a few politicians, bureaucrats, and journalists, we might add. What all these upset individuals seem to have forgotten is that, frequently, the best in the tradition of the humanities is thinking that was found disturbing when it was first published; this is because the vitality of the humanities derives from the creativity of human imagination and "the imagination is subversive. It endeavors to expose how things really are rather than how they are conventionally said to be, or it posits counterrealities, alternatives, utopias to the way things are."[30] Such counterviews constitute the signal legacy of every period of high humanistic achievement. In light of the extraordinary effervescence in intellectual activity marking the last half of this century, it seems indeed the case that "the theoretical and methodological battles waged within the humanities over the past two decades, despite obvious excesses and certain terroristic uses of 'theory,' represent a great renewal, indeed one that has brought us back to fundamental questions about the place of literature and culture in human life and society."[31] Postmodernism thus fits into a traditional pattern of renewal and continuity.

Moreover, contrary to the paranoid interpretation of some modernists, the humanities are not so much agents of change as its harbingers and, eventually, its interpreters. To promote the humanities is to create more opportunities to teach, discuss, and evaluate the issues raised by a reconsideration of all the fundamental questions evoked by the contemporary theoretical debates. Such a strategy derives from the realization "that the weaknesses of the humanities have been precisely the reverse of those of which they are usually accused. It is not that current theory subverts tradition, but that current theory has really been given no important place in the curriculum."[32] Fortunately, the defenders of the "true" humanities are being overtaken by events. Their efforts are negated by a zeitgeist that accounts for the fact that "the humanities are being saved outside themselves by new discourses that have developed within the last ten years: on the one hand what the French have called the *sciences humaines* including linguistics, structural anthropology and psychoanalysis, and on the other what we in the United States refer to as 'women's studies.' "[33]

If the purpose of intellectual work is still seen as an intention to disturb and disrupt, it is because we still subscribe to Kant's *sapere aude,* to the hope that desire for knowledge continues to be the best guarantee ensuring the survival and perpetuation of the human species. There is undeniable value in the legacy of the past, but the reality of the legacy is also determined by present needs and desires.

It is on the basis of these needs that our own values evolve. The Enlightenment was mainly enlightening for those who saw themselves emerging from the constraints of the ancien régime. We must forge our own Enlightenment with themes that relate to past experience, but these ideas must be shaped less by the authority of the canon than insights derived from the future perfect we must take as our ethical imperative. For our postmodern thought, this is a commitment that is, at the same time, the very reason for its existence. Postmodernism is also intrinsically prevented from achieving what it claims to be; and it is this discrepancy between an alleged essence and an actual effect that helps postmodern thinking renew its commitment every time it threatens to solidify into dogma, into a program designed to serve a particular age or cultural regime.

NOTES

INDEX

NOTES

Introduction

1. Dominique Janicaud, *La puissance du rationnel* (Paris: Gallimard, 1989), 12. All unattributed translations from the French are mine.

2. Cornel West, "Introduction," *Union Seminary Quarterly Review* 34, no. 2 (1979): 68.

3. Claude Julien, "Le risque et la raison," *Le Monde diplomatique* 440 (Nov. 1990): 6.

4. Michèle LeDœuff, *The Philosophical Imaginary,* trans. Colin Gordon (Stanford: Stanford Univ. Press, 1989), 118.

5. Larry Ray, "Foucault, Critical Theory and the Decomposition of the Historical Subject," *Philosophy and Social Criticism* 14, no. 1 (1988): 80, 85.

6. Hervé Hamon and Patrick Rotman, *Génération: I Les années de rêve* (Paris: Seuil, 1987), 262, 263.

7. Kenneth Liberman, "Decentering the Self: Two Perspectives from Philosophical Anthropology," in *The Question of the Other: Essays in Contemporary Continental Philosophy,* ed. Arleen B. Dallery and Charles E. Scott (Albany: State Univ. of New York Press, 1989), 128.

8. Thomas R. Thorp, "Derrida and Habermas on the Subject of Political Philosophy," in *Crises in Continental Philosophy,* ed. Arleen B. Dallery and Charles E. Scott with P. Holley Roberts (Albany: State Univ. of New York Press, 1990), 89. I return to this debate in chapter 4.

9. Thomas Docherty, *After Theory: Postmodernism/Postmarxism* (London: Routledge, 1990), 211.

10. T. Carlos Jacques, "Whence Does the Critic Speak? A Study of Foucault's Genealogy," *Philosophy and Social Criticism* 17 (1991): 332.

11. Michel Foucault, "What Is Enlightenment?" *The Foucault Reader,* ed. Paul Rabinow (New York: Pantheon, 1984), 49.

12. David R. Shumway, *Michel Foucault* (Boston: Twayne, 1989), 113.

13. Zygmunt Bauman, *Legislators and Interpreters: On Modernity, Post-Modernity and Intellectuals* (Ithaca: Cornell Univ. Press, 1987), 148.

14. Barry Smart, *Foucault, Marxism and Critique* (London: Routledge and Kegan Paul, 1983), 116.

15. Jane Flax, "Postmodernism and Gender Relations in Feminist Theory," in *Feminism/Postmodernism,* ed. Linda J. Nicholson (New York and London: Routledge, 1990), 43.

16. As Meyer shows, this fallacy was already detected by Leibnitz, who

found that "to say *I think, therefore I am,* does not really amount to proving existence through thought, since to think and to be thinking is the same thing; and to say *I am thinking,* is already to say: *I am.*" Indeed, Meyer points out, "I am" as soon as "I am thinking"; these are hardly two distinct moments of cogitation and the idea that one founds the other is but a rhetorical trick, an illusion made possible by grammar (Michel Meyer, *De la problématologie: Philosophie, science et langage* [Brussels: Pierre Mardaga, 1986], 198). I discuss Meyer's own elaboration of this theme in chapter 2.

17. Mark C. Taylor, "Descartes, Nietzsche and the Search for the Unsayable," *New York Times Book Review,* Feb. 1, 1987, 3.

18. Meyer, *De la problématologie,* 136.

19. Gianni Vattimo, *The End of Modernity: Nihilism and Hermeneutics in Postmodern Culture,* trans. Jon R. Snyder (Baltimore: Johns Hopkins Univ. Press, 1990), 169.

20. Ibid., 9.

Chapter 1

1. Roland Barthes, "Le dernier des écrivains heureux," in Voltaire, *Romans et Contes* (Paris: Seuil, 1964), 9–17.

2. Ibid., 17.

3. Roland Barthes, "Authors and Writers," *Critical Essays* (Evanston: Northwestern Univ. Press, 1972), p. 146.

4. Roland Barthes, *Critique et vérité* (Paris: Seuil, 1966), 74.

5. Barthes, "Le dernier des écrivains heureux," 16.

6. Luc Ferry and Alain Renaut, *La pensée 68: Essai sur l'anti-humanisme contemporain* (Paris: Gallimard, 1985). In English: *French Philosophy of the Sixties: An Essay on Antihumanism,* trans. Mary Schnackenberg Cattani (Amherst: Univ. of Massachusetts Press, 1990).

7. Jacques Bouveresse, *Rationalité et cynisme* (Paris: Minuit, 1984), 17, 15. Bouveresse's book is in part a tribute to Peter Sloterdijk, whose book *Kritik der zynischen Vernunft* (Frankfurt am Main: Suhrkamp Verlag, 1983) was an enormous bestseller in Germany. Bouveresse's commentary neglects the question of the agenda structuring the concerns of a generation of German writers obsessed with exorcising the specter of a recent national experience.

8. "Jean-Paul Sartre répond," *L'Arc* 30 (1966): 30. Henri Lefebvre and Dominique Lecourt, among others, made similar comments.

9. Jean-Paul Aron, *Les modernes* (Paris: Gallimard, 1984), 200–206.

10. Philip Lewis makes this point quite convincingly, I believe, in his article "The Post-structuralist Condition," *Diacritics* 12 (1982): 2–24.

11. Pierre Bourdieu, *Homo academicus* (Paris: Minuit, 1984), 281.

12. Jonathan Culler, "Problems in the History of Contemporary Criticism," *Journal of the Midwest Modern Language Association* 17 (1984): 3.

13. Arnold Beichman, "Is Higher Education in the Dark Ages?" *New York Times Magazine,* Nov. 6, 1983, 87. At the time of the article's publication, the writer was a visiting fellow at the Hoover Institution on War, Revolution and Peace.

14. The article is by syndicated columnist Mona Charen and appeared on Sept. 3, 1990. The books are by Alan Bloom, Peter Shaw, and Roger Kimball.

15. Comments made at the conference "The Ends of the Humanities: Redefinitions" at Miami University on Oct. 21–23, 1984. The title of Bennett's special address was "The Humanities: The Problem Isn't Redefinition."

16. Carl E. Schorske, "Secretary Bennett and His Conservative Supporters Are the New Fundamentalists of Western Culture," *Chronicle of Higher Education,* June 1, 1988, B1.

17. Alan Riding, "Europe's Future Hangs on the French Voter's Whim," *New York Times,* Sept. 13, 1992, E5.

18. Peter Brooks, "Western Civilization at Bay," *TLS,* Jan. 25, 1991, 5.

19. Fred Dallmayr, "Politics and Conceptual Analysis: Comments on Vollrath," *Philosophy and Social Criticism* 13 (1987): 34.

20. Claude Lefort, *Psychanalystes: Revue du Collège de Psychanalystes* 9 (Oct. 1983): 42, quoted in Bernard Flynn, "Claude Lefort: Political Forms of Modern Society," *Philosophy and Social Criticism* 13 (1987): 94.

21. Gianni Vattimo, *La société transparente* (Paris: Desclée de Brouver, 1990), 17.

22. Maurice Nadeau, "La Gauche en question," *La Quinzaine littéraire,* Aug. 1–31, 1984, 3. Peter Brooks attributes this idea to Jean Jaurès.

23. Michael Löwy, "La crise des intellectuels de gauche," *La Quinzaine littéraire,* Aug. 1–31, 1984, 33.

24. I have examined this strategy in the work of Foucault, specifically, in *Michel Foucault and the Subversion of Intellect* (Ithaca: Cornell Univ. Press, 1983).

25. Jacques Derrida, "The Principle of Reason: The University in the Eyes of Its Pupils," *Diacritics* 13 (1983): 18–19.

26. Ibid., 10.

27. Jacques Lacan, *Le Séminaire, Livre II: Le Moi dans la théorie de Freud et dans la technique de la psychanalyse* (Paris: Seuil, 1978), 231.

28. Derrida, "The Principle of Reason," 3.

Chapter 2

1. Jean Starobinski, *Montaigne in Motion,* trans. Arthur Goldhammer (Chicago: Univ. of Chicago Press, 1985), 293, 295.

2. Philip Lewis, "On Critics and Criticism," *French Review* 51 (1977): 254.

3. Maria Ruegg notes that "structuralism" referred . . . not only to those who called themselves, at one time or another, 'structuralist' (Lévi-Strauss, Barthes, Genette, Todorov), but also to those who explicitly disavowed the label (Foucault), to those who gave it only passing reference (Lacan, Althusser) and to those who openly attacked it (Derrida). In other words, it referred to what would later be recognized and identified—après coup—as 'poststructuralism'" ("The End(s) of French Style: Structuralism and Post-Structuralism in the American Context," *Criticism* 21 [1979]: 195).

4. Mark Poster, *Critical Theory and Poststructuralism: In Search of a Context* (Ithaca: Cornell Univ. Press, 1989), 4.

5. Charles Taylor, *Sources of the Self: The Making of the Modern Identity* (Cambridge: Harvard Univ. Press, 1989), 520.

6. Ibid., 367, 520.

7. Ibid., 152, 518.

8. Ibid., 519, 99.

9. Michel Foucault, "What Is Enlightenment?" *The Foucault Reader,* 45–46.

10. Taylor, *Sources of the Self,* 367.

11. Michel Rybalka, "Michel Foucault, Philosopher of Exclusion," *Contemporary French Civilization* 9 (1985): 197–98.

12. John Kenneth Galbraith, *The Culture of Contentment* (Boston: Houghton Mifflin, 1992), 2.

13. Sarah Kofman, "Descartes Entrapped," *Who Comes after the Subject?* ed. Eduardo Cadava, Peter Connor, and Jean-Luc Nancy (New York and London: Routledge, 1991), 182.

14. Friedrich Nietzsche, *Nachgelassene Fragmente* (1885), quoted in Kofman, "Descartes Entrapped," 178.

15. Ibid., 187–88.

16. Meyer, *De la problématologie,* 198.

17. Peter A. Schouls, *Descartes and the Enlightenment* (Edinburgh: Edinburgh Univ. Press, 1989), 45.

18. Meyer, *De la problématologie,* 185, 191.

19. Ibid., 140.

20. Kofman, "Descartes Entrapped," 183.

21. Ibid.

22. Ibid., 184–85.

23. Toril Moi, *Sexual/Textual Politics* (London: Methuen, 1985), 10.

24. Gary J. Handwerk, *Irony and Ethics in Narrative* (New Haven: Yale Univ. Press, 1985), 128–29.

25. Ibid., 168.

26. Ibid., 158–59.

27. Jacques Lacan, *Le Séminaire, Livre III: Les psychoses* (Paris: Seuil, 1981), 309.

28. Jacques Lacan, *Ecrits* (Paris: 1966), 867–68.

29. Lacan, *Le Séminaire, Livre II,* 112.

30. Handwerk, *Irony and Ethics in Narrative,* 166.

31. Jacques Lacan, "Of Structure as an Inmixing of an Otherness Prerequisite to Any Subject Whatever," in *The Structuralist Controversy,* ed. Richard Macksey and Eugenio Donato (Baltimore: Johns Hopkins Univ. Press, 1970), 121–22.

32. Handwerk, *Irony and Ethics in Narrative,* 167.

33. Jacques Lacan, *Television,* trans. Denis Hollier, Rosalind Krauss, and Annette Michelson (New York, London: Norton, 1990), 32.

34. Ibid., 32–33.

Chapter 3

1. Michel Foucault, *Remarks on Marx: Conversations with Duccio Trombadori,* trans. R. James Goldstein and James Cascaito (New York: Semiotext(e), 1991), 56.

2. Michel Foucault, "What Is Enlightenment," *The Foucault Reader,* 45–46.

3. Gayle L. Ormiston and Alan D. Schrift, Editors' Introduction, *The Hermeneutic Tradition: From Ast to Ricoeur* (Albany: State Univ. of New York Press, 1990), 2.

4. Michel Foucault, "The Ethic of Care for the Self as a Practice of Freedom," in *The Final Foucault,* ed. James Bernauer and David Rasmussen (Cambridge: MIT Press, 1988), 10.

5. Michel Foucault, "What Is Enlightenment," *The Foucault Reader,* 46.

6. Michel Foucault, "Archéologie d'une passion," *Magazine littéraire* 221 (July–Aug. 1985): 104. Interview with Foucault conducted by Charles Ruas.

7. Michel Foucault, *The Use of Pleasure,* trans. Robert Hurley (New York: Pantheon, 1985), 8.

8. Michel Foucault, *The Archaeology of Knowledge,* trans. A. M. Sheridan Smith (New York: Pantheon), 209.

9. Michel Foucault, *Radioscopie de Jacques Chancel,* Cassettes Radio France (Mar. 3, 1975). Interview with Foucault.

10. Foucault, *Remarks on Marx,* 33, 37.

11. Ibid., 38.

12. Michel Foucault, *Discipline and Punish: The Birth of the Prison,* trans. Alan Sheridan (New York: Vintage Books, 1979), 30.

13. Michel Foucault, *The Order of Things* (New York: Random House, 1970), 353.

14. Ibid., p. 323.

15. Michel Foucault, "La pensée du dehors," *Critique* 229 (1966): 530.

16. Foucault, *The Order of Things,* 342.

17. Raymond Bellour, *Le livre des autres* (Paris: U.G.E., 1978), 15. Interview with Foucault conducted in 1967.

18. Foucault, "Archéologie d'une passion," 105.

19. Foucault, *Radioscopie de Jacques Chancel.*

20. Michel Foucault, "Du pouvoir," *L'Express,* 13 July 1984, 56. Interview by Pierre Boncenne.

21. Michel Foucault, "Le souci de la vérité," *Magazine littéraire* 207 (May 1984): 18, 21. Interview by François Ewald.

22. Ibid., 18.

23. Michel Foucault, "How We Behave," *Vanity Fair,* Nov. 1983, 63. Interview by Paul Rabinow and Hubert L. Dreyfus.

24. Ibid., 66.

25. Ibid., 62.

26. Michel Foucault, "Final Interview," *Raritan* 5 (Summer 1985): 12. Interview by Gilles Barbadette and André Scala.

27. Foucault, "Le souci de la vérité," 22.

28. Ibid.

29. Foucault, "Du pouvoir," 60.

30. Foucault, "How We Behave," 62.

31. Eve Tavor Bannet, *Structuralism and the Logic of Dissent: Barthes, Derrida, Foucault, Lacan* (Urbana: Univ. of Illinois Press, 1989), 8, 95.

32. Gérard Raulet, "Structuralism and Post-Structuralism: An Interview with Michel Foucault," *Telos* 55 (Spring 1983), 202.

33. Bannet, *Structuralism and the Logic of Dissent,* 163.

34. Afterword: "The Subject and Power," in Hubert L. Dreyfus and Paul Rabinow, *Michel Foucault: Beyond Structuralism and Hermeneutics,* 2d ed. (Chicago: Univ. of Chicago Press, 1983), 231.

35. Bannet, *Structuralism and the Logic of Dissent,* 235.

36. Michel Foucault, "Nietzsche, Genealogy, History," in *Language, Counter-Memory, Practice,* ed. Donald F. Bouchard (Ithaca: Cornell Univ. Press, 1977), 163.

37. Foucault, *Remarks on Marx,* 18. James Miller's monumental study *The Passion of Michel Foucault* (New York: Simon and Schuster, 1993) was published when my book was already in press. Clearly, any discussion of Foucault's understanding of the self will henceforth have to take into account Miller's impressively argued thesis explaining Foucault's work in terms of his life. My own approach has been to take Foucault's pronouncements at their face value: that is, as insights that help elucidate the cultural and political existence of individuals in Western societies, and not as the manifestation of deep-seated obsessions or unconscious motivations that would help define the essential truth of a man called Michel Foucault.

Chapter 4

1. Michel Foucault, "Interview with Lucette Finas," in *Michel Foucault: Power, Truth, Strategy,* ed. Meaghan Morris and Paul Patton (Sidney: Feral Publications, 1979), 74–75.

2. Michel Foucault, "Politics and Ethics: An Interview," in *The Foucault Reader,* 374.

3. David Couzens Hoy, Introduction, in *Foucault: A Critical Reader,* ed. Hoy (Oxford: Basil Blackwell, 1986), 1. The book contains essays by Hoy, Ian Hacking, Richard Rorty, Michael Walzer, Charles Taylor, Jürgen Habermas, Hubert L. Dreyfus and Paul Rabinow, Edward Said, Barry Smart, Martin Jay, Mark Poster, and Arnold I. Davidson.

4. Charles Taylor, "Foucault on Freedom and Truth," in *Foucault: A Critical Reader,* 87, 88, 90 (emphasis original).

5. Ibid., 92 (emphasis original).

6. Ibid., 83.

7. Michael Walzer, "The Politics of Michel Foucault," in *Foucault: A Critical Reader,*. 62.

8. Sheldon S. Wolin, "On the Theory and Practice of Power," in *After Foucault: Humanistic Knowledge, Postmodern Challenges,* ed. Jonathan Arac (New Brunswick, N.J., Rutgers Univ. Press, 1988), 182–83.

9. Charles E. Scott, *The Question of Ethics: Nietzsche, Foucault, Heidegger* (Bloomington: Indiana Univ. Press, 1990), 61.

10. Foucault, *Remarks on Marx,* 62.

11. David R. Hiley, "Foucault and the Question of Enlightenment, *Philosophy and Social Criticism* 11 (1985): 74.

12. Michel Foucault, "Space, Knowledge, and Power," in *The Foucault Reader,* 249.

13. Walzer, "The Politics of Michel Foucault," in *Foucault: A Critical Reader,* 59.

14. Ibid., 61.

15. Michel Foucault, "Politics and Ethics: An Interview," in *The Foucault Reader*, 375.

16. Ian Hacking, "The Archaeology of Foucault," in *Foucault: A Critical Reader*, 39–40.

17. James W. Bernauer, *Michel Foucault's Force of Flight: Toward an Ethics for Thought* (Atlantic Highlands, N.J.: Humanities Press, 1990), 13.

18. John Rajchman, *Philosophical Events: Essays of the '80s* (New York: Columbia Univ. Press, 1991), 27, 38.

19. Ernst Behler, *Irony and the Discourse of Modernity* (Seattle: Univ. of Washington Press, 1990), 15–16.

20. Kofman, "Descartes Entrapped," 193–94.

21. Thorp, "Derrida and Habermas," 104.

22. Foucault, *Remarks on Marx*, 70.

23. Scott, *The Question of Ethics*, 60.

24. Hubert L. Dreyfus and Paul Rabinow, "What Is Maturity? Habermas and Foucault on 'What Is Enlightenment?' " in *Foucault: A Critical Reader*, 120.

25. Michael Walzer, "The Politics of Michel Foucault," in *Foucault: A Critical Reader*, 67.

26. Bernauer, *Michel Foucault's Force of Flight*, 33.

27. Ibid., 19, 110.

28. Rajchman, *Philosophical Events*, 20.

29. Scott, *The Question of Ethics*, 60.

30. Ibid., 5.

31. Ibid., 2.

32. Arnold I. Davidson, "Archaeology, Genealogy, Ethics," in *Foucault: A Critical Reader*, 222.

33. Ian Hacking, "The Archaeology of Foucault," in *Foucault: A Critical Reader*, 30.

34. Hoy, Introduction, in *Foucault: A Critical Reader*, 12, 17.

35. Scott, *The Question of Ethics*, 10.

36. Ibid., 81.

37. Ibid.

38. Ibid., 5.

39. Ibid., 92, 86.

40. Ibid., 91, 88.

41. Barry Smart, "The Politics of Truth and the Problem of Hegemony," in *Foucault: A Critical Reader*, 162.

42. David Couzens Hoy, "Power, Repression, Progress: Foucault, Lukes, and the Frankfurt School," in *Foucault: A Critical Reader*, 139.

43. Bernauer, *Michel Foucault's Force of Flight*, 174.

44. Ibid., 166.

45. Ibid., 4.

46. Ibid., 10, 11.

47. Ibid., 6.

Chapter 5

1. John McGowan, *Postmodernism and Its Critics* (Ithaca: Cornell Univ. Press, 1991), 13.

2. Jean-François Revel, *Ni Marx ni Jésus: La nouvelle révolution mondiale est commencée aux Etats-Unis* (Paris, Robert Laffont, 1970), 204.

3. Vattimo, *La société transparente*, 57.

4. Roy Boyne, *Foucault and Derrida: The Other Side of Reason* (London: Unwin Hyman, 1990), 154.

5. Barry Smart, "Modernity, Postmodernity and the Present," in *Theories of Modernity and Postmodernity,* ed. Bryan S. Turner (London: Sage, 1990), 27.

6. Linda Hutcheon, *The Politics of Postmodernism* (London: Routledge, 1989), 2.

7. Foucault, "Space, Knowledge, and Power," in *The Foucault Reader*, 249.

8. Barbara Becker-Cantarino, "Foucault on Kant: Deconstructing the Enlightenment," in *The Enlightenment and Its Legacy: Studies in German Literature in Honor of Helga Slessarev,* ed. Sara Friedrichsmeyer and Becker-Cantarino (Bonn: Bouvier Verlag, 1991), 31.

9. Dreyfus and Rabinow, "What Is Maturity?" in *Foucault: A Critical Reader,* 111.

10. Foucault, "Un cours inédit," *Magazine littéraire* 207 (May 1984): 39.

11. Foucault, "What Is Enlightenment?" in *The Foucault Reader*, 45, 42–43.

12. Norman Suckling, "The Unfulfilled Renaissance: An Essay on the Fortunes of Enlightened Humanism in the 18th Century," *Studies on Voltaire and the Eighteenth Century* 86 (1971): 87.

13. Michel Foucault, "Two Lectures," in *Power/Knowledge: Selected Interviews and Other Writings, 1972–1977,* ed. Colin Gordon (New York: Pantheon, 1980), 93.

14. Ibid., 106.

15. Boyne, *Foucault and Derrida,* 121.

16. Foucault, "Two Lectures," 106.

17. Ibid., 107.

18. Hoy, Introduction, in *Foucault: A Critical Reader,* 23.

19. Michel Foucault, *Histoire de la folie à l'âge classique* (Paris: Gallimard, 1972), 368.

20. Denis Diderot, *Rameau's Nephew and Other Works,* trans. Jacques Barzun and Ralph H. Bowen (Indianapolis: Bobbs-Merrill, 1964), 29.

21. Ibid., 38.

22. Ibid., 50.

23. Ibid., 33.

24. Ibid., 25.

25. Diderot, *Le neveu de Rameau: Satires, Contes et Entretiens,* ed. Jacques and Anne-Marie Chouillet (Paris: Le Livre de Poche, 1984), 207.

26. Wilda Anderson, *Diderot's Dream* (Baltimore: Johns Hopkins Univ. Press, 1990), 254.

27. Diderot, "Entretien d'un philosophe avec la maréchale de xxx," in *Le neveu de Rameau,* 322.

28. "Supplément au voyage de Bougainville ou dialogue entre A et B sur l'inconvénient d'attacher des idées morales à certaines actions physiques qui n'en comportent pas," in *Le neveu de Rameau,* 265.

29. Cornelius Castoriadis, "The Nature and Value of Equality," *Philosophy and Social Criticism* 11 (1986): 383, 385.

30. Todd May, "Is Post-Structuralist Political Theory Anarchist?" *Philosophy and Social Criticism* 15 (1989): 171.

31. John Rajchman, *Michel Foucault: The Freedom of Philosophy* (New York: Columbia Univ. Press, 1985), 105.

32. Georges Balandier, *Le détour: pouvoir et modernité* (Paris: Fayard, 1985), 147.

33. Michel Foucault, "Practicing Criticism," in *Michel Foucault: Politics, Philosophy, Culture: Interviews and Other Writings, 1977–1984,* ed. Lawrence D. Kritzman (New York: Routledge, 1988), 155.

34. Michel Foucault, "The Minimalist Self," in *Michel Foucault: Politics,* 14.

35. Foucault, "Practicing Criticism," in *Michel Foucault: Politics,* 155.

36. Bernauer, *Michel Foucault's Force of Flight,* 157.

37. Foucault, "What Is Enlightenment," in *The Foucault Reader,* 42.

Chapter 6

1. Renée Waldinger, ed. *Approaches to Teaching Voltaire's Candide* (New York: Modern Language Association of America, 1987).

2. Hutcheon, *The Politics of Postmodernism,* 26.

3. Suckling, "The Unfulfilled Renaissance," 37.

4. Bernhard Waldenfels, "Experience of the Other: Between Appropriation and Disappropriation," in *Life-World and Politics,* ed. Stephen K. White (Notre Dame: Univ. of Notre Dame Press, 1989), 66.

5. Boyne, *Foucault and Derrida,* 33.

6. Cornelius Castoriadis, *Le monde morcelé: Les carrefours du labyrinthe III* (Paris: Seuil, 1990), 13.

7. Francis Fukuyama, "The End of History?" *National Interest* (Summer 1989), 3–18. For Fukuyama, this self-fulfillment of modernity is marked by "an unabashed victory of economic and political liberalism" (3).

8. Chantal Mouffe, "Radical Democracy: Modern or Postmodern?" In *Universal Abandon? The Politics of Postmodernism,* ed. Andrew Ross (Minneapolis: Univ. of Minnesota Press, 1988), 40.

9. David R. Hiley, "Foucault and the Question of Enlightenment," 63.

10. Max Horkheimer, *The Eclipse of Reason* (New York: Seabury Press, 1974), 26.

11. Andreas Huyssen, "Mapping the Postmodern," in *Feminism/Postmodernism,* 236.

12. Andrew Ross, Introduction, in *Universal Abandon?* xii.

13. Quoted in Mouffe, "Radical Democracy," 35.

14. William E. Connolly, *Political Theory and Modernity* (Oxford: Basil Blackwell, 1988), 3. Michel Foucault's discussion of the "analytic of finitude" is to be found in *The Order of Things.*

15. David Couzens Hoy, "Foucault: Modern or Postmodern?" In *After Foucault,* 25.

16. Irene Diamond, "Babies, Heroic Experts, and a Poisoned Earth," in *Reweaving the World: The Emergence of Ecofeminism,* ed. Irene Diamond and Gloria Feman Orenstein (San Francisco: Sierra Club, 1990), 210.

17. Bernauer, *Michel Foucault's Force of Flight,* 45, 156.
18. Pierre Bayle, *Œuvres diverses* (Paris: Editions sociales, 1971), 77.
19. Albert Camus, *The Rebel: An Essay on Man in Revolt,* trans. Anthony Bower (New York: Knopf, 1961), 131.
20. Ray, "Foucault, Critical Theory and the Decomposition of the Historical Subject," 80.
21. Castoriadis, "The Nature and Value of Equality," 381.
22. Calvin O. Schrag, "Rationality between Modernity and Postmodernity," in *Life-World and Politics,* 88.
23. Roy Porter, *The Enlightenment* (Atlantic Highlands, N.J.: Humanities Press, 1990), 71.
24. Mouffe, "Radical Democracy," 32. Mouffe credits Blumenberg and Rorty with this idea.
25. Ibid., 37.
26. Horkheimer, *The Eclipse of Reason,* 63.
27. Foucault, *Remarks on Marx,* 159.
28. Fred. R. Dallmayr, "Life-World: Variations on a Theme," in *Life-World and Politics,* 59.
29. Mouffe, "Radical Democracy," 36.
30. Gayle L. Ormiston, "Postmodern *Différends,*" in *Crises in Continental Philosophy,* 237.
31. Jean-François Lyotard, *Le postmoderne expliqué aux enfants: Correspondance 1982–1985* (Paris: Galilée, 1986), 123. Lyotard uses the word *relever,* which is literally closer to *aufheben* than "integrate," the term I use to signify the process of dialectical overcoming.
32. Patrick Henry, "Contre Barthes," *Studies on Voltaire and the Eighteenth Century* 249 (1987), 31.
33. John Weightman, "Cultivating Voltaire," *New York Review of Books,* 18 June 1970, 37, quoted by Henry, "Contre Barthes," 32.

Chapter 7

1. Michel Henri, *La barbarie* (Paris: Grasset, 1987), 241.
2. George F. Kennan, *Sketches from a Life* (New York: Pantheon, 1989), 364–65.
3. Bannet, *Structuralism and the Logic of Dissent,* 156.
4. Franco Crespi, *Médiation symbolique et société,* trans. Crespi and Françoise Marie Rizzi (Paris: Méridiens, 1983), 108.
5. *Chronicle of Higher Education,* Nov. 8, 1989, A22.
6. Peter Fuller, "Towards a New Nature for the Gothic," *Art and Design* (1987): 6. Special issue on "The Postmodern Object."
7. Barbara Herrnstein Smith, *Contingencies of Value* (Cambridge: Harvard Univ. Press, 1988), 181.
8. Hilton Kramer, "Studying the Arts and the Humanities: What Can Be Done?" *New Criterion* 7 (Feb. 1989): 3.
9. Sidney Hook, "The Barbarism of Virtue," *PMLA* 84 (1969): 466, 469.
10. Sidney Hook, "Civilization and Its Malcontents," *The National Review,* Oct. 13, 1989, 32–33.

11. Smith, *Contingencies of Value,* 73–74.

12. Richard Ohmann, *Politics of Letters* (Middletown, Conn.: Wesleyan Univ. Press, 1987), 186.

13. Claude Lefort, *Democracy and Political Theory,* trans. David Macey (Cambridge: Polity Press, 1988), 18.

14. David Couzens Hoy, "Foucault: Modern or Postmodern?" in *After Foucault,* 34.

15. Jacques Donzelot, "Nouveaux mécanismes," *Esprit* 11 (Nov. 1987): 30–41.

16. Ohmann, *Politics of Letters,* 192.

17. Bernauer, *Michel Foucault's Force of Flight,* 33.

18. Castoriadis, "The Nature and Value of Equality," 374.

19. Smith, *Contingencies of Value,* 160, 161, 177.

20. Ibid., 183.

21. Hoy, "Foucault: Modern or Postmodern?" 29.

22. Smith, *Contingencies of Value,* 95.

23. Romain Laufer and Catherine Paradeise, *Le prince bureaucrate: Machiavel au pays du marketing* (Paris: Flammarion, 1982), 190.

24. Ibid., 30–31.

25. Lefort, *Democracy and Political Theory,* 154.

26. *Nouvelle histoire des idées politiques,* Pascal Ory, ed. (Paris: Hachette, 1987), 577.

27. Laufer and Paradeise, *Le prince bureaucrate,* 61.

28. Guy Hocquenghem and René Schérer, *L'âme atomique: Pour une esthétique d'ère nucléaire* (Paris: Albin Michel, 1986), 19.

29. Laufer and Paradeise, *Le prince bureaucrate,* 190.

30. Hocquenghem and Schérer, *L'âme atomique,* 19.

31. Laufer and Paradeise, *Le prince bureaucrate,* 172.

32. Ibid., 173.

33. Ibid., 113.

34. Lewis H. Lapham, *Money and Class in America: Notes and Observations on Our Civil Religion* (New York: Weidenfeld and Nicholson, 1988), 180. The comments are those of Senator Daniel P. Moynihan.

35. Laufer and Paradeise, *Le prince bureaucrate,* 35.

36. Lapham, *Money and Class in America,* 21.

37. Steven J. Bartlett, "Philosophy as Ideology," *Metaphilosophy* 17 (Jan. 1986): 10.

38. James S. Coleman, *The Asymmetric Society* (Syracuse: Syracuse Univ. Press, 1982), 6.

39. Lapham, *Money and Class in America,* 36.

40. Ibid., 6.

41. Ibid., 235.

42. Coleman, *The Asymmetric Society,* 26.

43. Stanley Aronowitz, "Postmodernism and Politics," *Social Text* 18 (Winter 1987): 105.

44. Claude Lefort, *Democracy and Political Theory,* 17–18.

45. Ibid., 16.

46. Ibid., 19.

47. Ibid., 11.

Chapter 8

1. Foucault, *Remarks on Marx,* 69–70.

2. Michel Foucault, "Human Nature: Justice versus Power," in *Reflexive Water: The Basic Concerns of Mankind,* ed. Fons Elders (London: Souvenir Press, 1974), 149.

3. Betty Jean Craige, *Reconnection: Dualism to Holism in Literary Study* (Athens: Univ. of Georgia Press, 1988), 78–79.

4. Shoshana Felman, "Psychoanalysis and Education: Teaching Terminable and Interminable," *Yale French Studies* 63 (1982): 28.

5. Patrick Brantlinger, *Crusoe's Footprints: Cultural Studies in Britain and America* (New York: Routledge, 1990), 7.

6. George Levine, "Graff Revisited," *Raritan* 8 (1989): 121.

7. *The Humanities in American Life,* Report of the Commission on the Humanities (Berkeley: Univ. of California Press, 1980), 2.

8. Ibid., 3.

9. Frank H. T. Rhodes, "Reforming Higher Education Will Take More than Just Tinkering with Curricula," *Chronicle of Higher Education,* May 22, 1985, 80.

10. *Humanities in American Life,* 4.

11. William J. Bennett, "The Shattered Humanities," *Wall Street Journal,* 31 Dec. 1982, 10.

12. Lynne V. Cheney, "Students of Success," *Newsweek,* Sept. 1, 1986, 7.

13. *Toward the Year 2000: A Focused Agenda for Ohio,* vol. 2 (Ohio Board of Regents, Sept. 8, 1988), 28.

14. William J. Bennett, quoted in "Note Pad," *Chronicle of Higher Education,* May 22, 1985, 23.

15. Jean-François Lyotard, *The Postmodern Condition: A Report on Knowledge,* trans. Geoff Bennington and Brian Massumi (Minneapolis: Univ. of Minnesota Press, 1984), 34–35.

16. If this is indeed the case, then the current situation would seem to stand in direct contrast with another highly influential historical antecedent, that of the classical ideal of schooling found in Greek and Roman tradition. The word *school,* which is *skole* in Greek and *scola* in Latin, meant "leisure"; *a-scolia* denoted "business." Similarly, in Latin *otium* was "laziness" or "studied leisure," its opposite being *negotium,* or "business." This opposition is also the source of the later, medieval distinction between *artes liberales* and *artes serviles.* What is ironic in the present situation is the apparent tendency to make liberal arts useful for business, to convert *otium* into its negation, into *negotium.*

17. "Text of Cheney's 'Report to the President, the Congress, and the American People' on the Humanities in America," *Chronicle of Higher Education,* Sept. 21, 1988, A17.

18. Burton J. Bledstein, *The Culture of Professionalism: The Middle Class and the Development of Higher Education in America* (New York: Norton, 1976), x.

19. Helen Lefkowitz Horowitz, "Why So Many Students Today Are 'Grinds,'" *Chronicle of Higher Education,* Jan. 8, 1986, 112.

20. Jerry Herron, *Universities and the Myth of Cultural Decline* (Detroit: Wayne State Univ. Press, 1988), 32.

21. Craige, *Reconnection,* 67.

22. Jay Parini, "Academic Conservatives Who Decry 'Politicization' Show Staggering Naïveté about Their Own Biases," *Chronicle of Higher Education,* Dec. 7, 1988, 81.

23. Donald Lazere, "Conservative Critics Have a Distorted View of What Constitutes Ideological Bias in Academe," *Chronicle of Higher Education,* Nov. 9, 1988, A52.

24. Felman, "Psychoanalysis and Education," 28–29.

25. John D. Caputo, "Disseminating Originary Ethics and the Ethics of Dissemination," in *The Question of the Other,* 57–58. Moreover, as Gerald Graff demonstrates, the canon turns out to be much less inflexible than its name would imply and has adapted itself quite readily to the cultural and political needs of various historical periods. See *Beyond the Culture Wars: How Teaching the Conflicts Can Revitalize American Education* (New York: Norton, 1992).

26. Jacques, "Whence Does the Critic Speak?" 344 n. 16.

27. McGowan, *Postmodernism and Its Critics,* 15.

28. Foucault, *Remarks on Marx,* 180.

29. Ibid., 34.

30. Felman, "Psychoanalysis and Education," 31.

31. Liberman, "Decentering the Self," 132.

Conclusion

1. Kofman, "Descartes Entrapped," 183.

2. Jeffrey Sammons, "Squaring the Circle: Observations on the Core Curriculum and the Plight of the Humanities," *Profession 86* (Modern Language Association of America, 1986), 15.

3. Zygmunt Bauman, *Legislators and Interpreters,* 188. In a similar manner, the government itself appears to be incapable of formulating its own rationales. The authors of a recent study of the American political system note that, following some major changes the Reagan administration implemented in a few areas of domestic and international policy, "drift and incoherence largely characterized American government during the balance of the 1980s" (Benjamin Ginsberg and Martin Shefter, *Politics by Other Means: The Declining Importance of Elections in America* [New York: Basic Books, 1990], 163).

4. Georges Balandier, *Le détour: pouvoir et modernité* (Paris: Fayard, 1985), 173. This contradiction is also reflected in one of Bennett's arguments. Bennett likes to maintain that our society has been shaped by the great ideas contained in the great books of Western civilization; yet, as Ohmann points out, "if one subscribes to idealist history, surely the shaping ideas of our society are rendered more accurately in such immortal words from the past as 'The business of America is business,' and 'What's good for General Motors is good for the country,' than by the ideas Bennett has in mind" (Ohmann,

Politics of Letters, p. 14). Of course, to recognize this would be to admit the fact of the manipulation—which is made all the more striking by the lack of effectiveness such slogans would have today.

5. A good example of this is the full-page ads taken out by the National Association of Scholars to outline the organization's stand on a number of issues. The NAS purports to encourage the study of the "achievements of other nations and of ethnic subcultures" but only by way of "generally applicable intellectual and aesthetic standards." These standards apparently lead it to recognize that "the truths of mathematics, the sciences, history, and so on, are not different for people of different races, sexes, or culture." Besides, the fact that others are adopting Western practices is deemed a sufficiently compelling "testament to the universality of [Western] values" (*Chronicle of Higher Education,* Nov. 8, 1989, A23).

6. Peter Brooks, "Western Civ at Bay," review of Allan Bloom, *Giants and Dwarfs: Essays 1960–1990* and Roger Kimball, *Tenured Radicals: How Politics Has Corrupted Our Higher Education, TLS,* Jan. 25, 1991, 6.

7. Sammons, "Squaring the Circle," 19.

8. Ohmann, *Politics of Letters,* 16.

9. Sammons, "Squaring the Circle," 17.

10. Ibid., 16.

11. Levine, "Graff Revisited," 122.

12. Brooks, "Western Civ at Bay," 6.

13. Neil Wilson, "Punching Out the Enlightenment: A Discussion of Peter Sloterdijk's *Kritik der zynischen Vernunft,*" *New German Critique* 41 (Spring–Summer 1987): 65. Wilson is referring to a point made by Kurt Wolff in "Surrender-and-Catch Hermeneutics," *Philosophy and Social Criticism* 1 (1984): 1–16.

14. Serge Viderman, *Le disséminaire* (Paris: PUF, 1987), 19.

15. Vattimo, *The End of Modernity,* xii.

16. Balandier, *Le détour,* 220.

17. Janicaud, *La puissance du rationnel,* 44.

18. Moi, *Sexual/Textual Politics,* 8.

19. Crespi, *Médiation symbolique et société,* 179.

Such an incapacity and insecurity in the face of the growing complexity of the real is noted by political commentators. Kevin Phillips writes: "From the White House to Capitol Hill, a critical weakness in American politics and governance is becoming woefully apparent—the frightening inability of the nation's leaders to face, much less define and debate, the unprecedented problems and opportunities facing the country" (*The Politics of Rich and Poor: Wealth and the American Electorate in the Reagan Aftermath* [New York: Random House, 1990], 23).

20. Vattimo, *The End of Modernity,* 169–70.

21. Lefort, *Democracy and Political Theory,* 80.

22. Crespi, *Médiation symbolique et société,* 152–53.

23. Docherty, *After Theory,* 213.

24. Jean-François Lyotard, *Tombeau de l'intellectuel et autres papiers* (Paris: Galilée, 1984), 22.

25. Bruce Robbins suggests that "we consider intellectuals as not in de-

cline, but as 'grounded.'" He understands the term in two senses: one meaning "to confine to quarters, to restrict the movement of," the other in the sense of "to base, to establish, to serve as the foundation of." Both senses correspond to a postmodern understanding of intellectual involvement; the scope of their ambition and activities finds itself greatly reduced and is indeed to be grounded in an institutional setting ("Intellectuals in Decline?" *Social Text* 25/26 [1990]: 258).

26. Vattimo, *The End of Modernity,* 47.

27. Foucault, "What Is Enlightenment?" in *The Foucault Reader,* 47.

28. Barthes, *Critical Essays,* p. 146. See chapter 1.

29. Richard Rorty, "Two Cheers for the Cultural Left," *South Atlantic Quarterly* 89 (Winter 1990): 227.

30. Sammons, "Squaring the Circle," 18.

31. Brooks, "Western Civ at Bay," 6.

32. Levine, "Graff Revisited," 133. The author is commenting on Gerald Graff's proposal for curricular innovations in the humanities. A recent and most persuasive restatement of this proposal is Graff's *Beyond the Culture Wars*.

33. Elaine Marks, "Breaking the Bread: Gestures toward Other Structures, Other Discourses," *Bulletin of the MMLA,* 13 (Spring 1980): 53.

Index